British Politics: A Very Short Introduction

VERY SHORT INTRODUCTIONS are for anyone wanting a stimulating and accessible way into a new subject. They are written by experts, and have been translated into more than 45 different languages.

The series began in 1995, and now covers a wide variety of topics in every discipline. The VSI library currently contains over 650 volumes—a Very Short Introduction to everything from Psychology and Philosophy of Science to American History and Relativity—and continues to grow in every subject area.

Very Short Introductions available now:

ABOLITIONISM Richard S. Newman
THE ABRAHAMIC RELIGIONS
    Charles L. Cohen
ACCOUNTING Christopher Nobes
ADAM SMITH Christopher J. Berry
ADOLESCENCE Peter K. Smith
ADVERTISING Winston Fletcher
AERIAL WARFARE Frank Ledwidge
AESTHETICS Bence Nanay
AFRICAN AMERICAN RELIGION
    Eddie S. Glaude Jr
AFRICAN HISTORY John Parker and
    Richard Rathbone
AFRICAN POLITICS Ian Taylor
AFRICAN RELIGIONS
    Jacob K. Olupona
AGEING Nancy A. Pachana
AGNOSTICISM Robin Le Poidevin
AGRICULTURE Paul Brassley and
    Richard Soffe
ALBERT CAMUS Oliver Gloag
ALEXANDER THE GREAT
    Hugh Bowden
ALGEBRA Peter M. Higgins
AMERICAN CULTURAL HISTORY
    Eric Avila
AMERICAN FOREIGN RELATIONS
    Andrew Preston
AMERICAN HISTORY Paul S. Boyer
AMERICAN IMMIGRATION
    David A. Gerber
AMERICAN LEGAL HISTORY
    G. Edward White
AMERICAN NAVAL HISTORY
    Craig L. Symonds

AMERICAN POLITICAL HISTORY
    Donald Critchlow
AMERICAN POLITICAL PARTIES
    AND ELECTIONS L. Sandy Maisel
AMERICAN POLITICS
    Richard M. Valelly
THE AMERICAN PRESIDENCY
    Charles O. Jones
THE AMERICAN REVOLUTION
    Robert J. Allison
AMERICAN SLAVERY
    Heather Andrea Williams
THE AMERICAN WEST Stephen Aron
AMERICAN WOMEN'S HISTORY
    Susan Ware
ANAESTHESIA Aidan O'Donnell
ANALYTIC PHILOSOPHY
    Michael Beaney
ANARCHISM Colin Ward
ANCIENT ASSYRIA Karen Radner
ANCIENT EGYPT Ian Shaw
ANCIENT EGYPTIAN ART AND
    ARCHITECTURE Christina Riggs
ANCIENT GREECE Paul Cartledge
THE ANCIENT NEAR EAST
    Amanda H. Podany
ANCIENT PHILOSOPHY Julia Annas
ANCIENT WARFARE Harry Sidebottom
ANGELS David Albert Jones
ANGLICANISM Mark Chapman
THE ANGLO-SAXON AGE John Blair
ANIMAL BEHAVIOUR
    Tristram D. Wyatt
THE ANIMAL KINGDOM
    Peter Holland

Available soon:

For more information visit our website

www.oup.com/vsi/

Tony Wright

BRITISH POLITICS

A Very Short Introduction

THIRD EDITION

OXFORD
UNIVERSITY PRESS

OXFORD
UNIVERSITY PRESS

Great Clarendon Street, Oxford, OX2 6DP,
United Kingdom

Oxford University Press is a department of the University of Oxford.
It furthers the University's objective of excellence in research, scholarship,
and education by publishing worldwide. Oxford is a registered trade mark of
Oxford University Press in the UK and in certain other countries

First edition published 2003
Second edition published 2013
This edition published 2020

Impression: 2

Published in the United States of America by Oxford University Press
198 Madison Avenue, New York, NY 10016, United States of America

British Library Cataloguing in Publication Data
Data available

Library of Congress Control Number: 2020930785

ISBN 978-0-19-882732-0

Printed in Great Britain by
Ashford Colour Press Ltd, Gosport, Hampshire

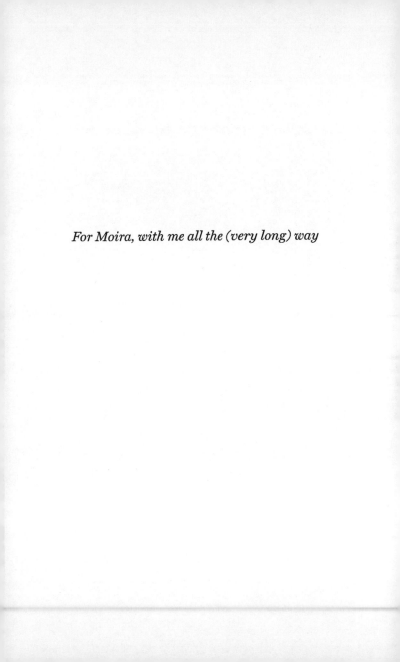

For Moira, with me all the (very long) way

Contents

Contents

Preface

Since the previous edition of this little book was published, there have been momentous changes in British politics. The most dramatic by far has been the referendum decision in 2016 to leave the European Union (soon known as 'Brexit'), the repercussions of which have dominated British politics in the years since and are still playing themselves out as I write (at the end of 2019) and will continue to do so for a long time in the future. This has required substantial rewriting, along with a new final chapter. I have tried to retain the character of the original, which is that of an extended essay rather than a textbook. It offers an overview, in which current events are placed within a longer and larger perspective. It is intended to be read by anyone with an interest in British politics, whether as student or citizen (or both).

This book was already in proof when the coronavirus pandemic arrived, testing the political system as never before in peacetime, bringing a massive extension of state action and with profound consequences for all aspects of British politics, economy and society. This came too late to be included here though; and any assessment of its lasting impact will have to wait for the next edition.

I have spent part of my working life as an academic teaching about British politics, and another part practising politics as a Member of Parliament. I have tried to bring insights from both these roles to this book. Inevitably it contains judgements and perceptions that are my own, but if these provoke challenge and discussion so much the better.

Tony Wright

List of illustrations

Chapter 1

The Britishness of British politics

Try this game. You have to fill in the blank.

> French wine
> Italian food
> German cars
> British —

Not easy, is it? One of my children suggested 'humour', but that could scarcely be a British gift to the world if nobody else can understand the joke. Another came up with 'language', which would be the obvious candidate except for the fact that it is not *English* but *British* that we are talking about (a characteristic confusion that it will be necessary to say something more about shortly). So (as my children put it) what's the clever-clog answer then?

For a long time a good case could be made for 'politics' or 'government', although (as we shall see) recent events have called this into question in dramatic fashion. It had long been held (and not just by the British) that Britain has displayed a particular approach to politics that has offered lessons to the world in making government work. 'This country's distinctive contribution to civilisation', proclaimed the *Daily Telegraph* at the end of the

1. 'envied and enviable…': Winston Churchill eulogizes Britain's political system (1945).

last century, 'has been the development of stable institutions of representative government' (19 December 1997). There is plenty to unpick in such a statement, but it faithfully echoes a long line of such judgements about the political genius and blessings of the British.

These judgements have been delivered by domestic voices and by foreign observers; by rhetorical politicians and by dispassionate scholars; and by radicals and conservatives. A quick sample might include the following. In 1865 the radical John Bright famously described the country as the 'Mother of Parliaments'. At the end of the Second World War, prime minister Winston Churchill (Figure 1) told the House of Commons:

> If it be true, as has been said, that every country gets the form of government it deserves, we may certainly flatter ourselves. The wisdom of our ancestors has led us to an envied and enviable

situation. We have the strongest Parliament in the world. We have the oldest, the most famous, the most secure, the most serviceable monarchy in the world. King and Parliament both rest safely and solidly upon the will of the people expressed by free and fair election on the basis of universal suffrage. Thus the system has long worked harmoniously, both in peace and in war.   (15 May 1945)

This was pushing it a bit (it had not always been harmonious and full universal suffrage had only existed since 1928), but it nevertheless reflected a widely shared view. In the 1950s André Mathiot, in his French study of British politics, described the British system as 'an enviable model of democratic government', while adding: 'One can only regret that it could not possibly be transplanted to any other country.' In their classic comparative study of democracies published in 1963, the American political scientists Almond and Verba identified Britain as the exemplar of a successful 'civic culture'. In similar vein the political scientist Richard Rose introduced his textbook on the politics of England (yes, England) with the observation that: 'just as Alexis de Tocqueville travelled to America in 1831 to seek the secrets of democracy, so one might journey to England to seek the secrets of stable, representative government'. You get the picture.

It is not difficult to see why the 'British model' (as it sometimes came to be called) acquired this status. After all, compared with most other societies in Europe, Britain had enjoyed a long and remarkable history of political stability in modern times. Just to take the last hundred years, while countries like France and Germany were regularly making and unmaking their political systems under the impact of war, occupation, extremism, violence, revolution, and tyranny, Britain stayed firmly on the path of parliamentary democracy. This was a remarkable achievement, especially in the turbulent circumstances of the first half of the 20th century. It merited a proper amount of self-congratulation about the unique political skills of the British and the working of its political system.

But, as ever, there is more to be said about the Britishness of British politics than this kind of traditional verdict allows for. Up until the time of the French Revolution at the end of the 18th century, it was Britain's revolutionary history that defined its political tradition; and 'the British had a European reputation, whether admired or abhorred, as a politically volatile people given to regicide and rebellion' (Lively and Lively, *Democracy in Britain: A Reader*). In the 17th century Britain was a pretty bloody place. The struggle for democracy was just that, a struggle. Britain came relatively late to (near) universal suffrage, only getting there in 1918 after the upheaval of war. It pioneered parliamentary government, but not parliamentary democracy. Nor has the modern period been without its share of turbulence and upheaval, at some moments acutely so. Indeed, in the 1970s the British model ceased to be the object of envy and emulation and came to be seen for a time as the European basket case, the home of a bitterly adversarial kind of politics that prevented effective policy-making and brought the country to its knees. 'One does not have to be a doom-monger', wrote the political scientist Anthony King in 1975, 'to sense that something is wrong with our polity as well as our economy.' This is a reminder of a larger point, that political stability of the British kind is not the same as policy success, as the post-war British economic record makes clear. The lines of connection, and disconnection, in this area are much more complex.

Then there is the Irish question, often conveniently forgotten when the eulogies to the British polity were being composed, which has periodically brought violence and terror (with over 3,000 people killed in 'the Troubles') into a political system celebrated for its orderly continuities. Northern Ireland with its sectarian divisions is the standing exception to any generalization about modern British politics, which is why it has often been dropped from the picture altogether—until it has exploded its way in again (most recently in relation to the exit from the EU)—and why the peace process and power-sharing rooted in the historic Good Friday Agreement of 1998 remains work in progress.

Yet this is just the most glaring example of a more general tendency among the British not to know or care about who they are. In part, at least, this is the luxury available to a settled people. It can also be myopia, or worse. The English have always been the worst offenders in this respect, oblivious to the nature of the multinational state of which they are the overwhelmingly dominant part (and routinely conflating England with Britain). This is why they have had trouble in coming to terms with devolution and have been slow to embrace it for themselves (although Brexit has been associated with the rise of an English nationalism). But the tendency is a general one. The terms 'England' and 'Britain', and 'Great Britain' and 'United Kingdom' (a term hardly used in pre-devolution times) are constantly used and misused by people who have no idea what they mean or how they are different, or what their historical provenance is. There can scarcely have been a state in which its citizens were so hopelessly muddled about where they lived.

As the historian Norman Davies puts it, in his epic account of *The Isles*:

> One of the most extraordinary aspects of the current scene lies in the number of citizens of the United Kingdom who do not appear to be familiar with the basic parameters of the state in which they live. They often do not know what it is called; they do not distinguish between the whole and the constituent parts; and they have never grasped the most elementary facts of its development. Confusion reigns on every hand.

A good example is accidentally provided by the American writer Bill Bryson, in his best-selling account of his journeying around

Britain. Searching for the grave of George Orwell in Nuneham Courtenay cemetery in Oxfordshire, he comes upon the grave of Asquith, who had been prime minister at the height of the British empire in the early 20th century. Bryson is surprised that the inscription on the headstone describes Asquith as having been prime minister of *England*. He should not have been surprised. This is entirely typical of the prevailing confusions and elisions. The opening sentence of D. L. Keir's standard work on *The Constitutional History of Modern Britain* reads: 'Continuity has been the dominant characteristic in the development of English government.' He might have added that confusion has been the dominant characteristic in descriptions of the British polity.

Yet the confusion is the reality. It can seem merely pedantic to try to hang on to some proper distinctions and definitions. That Britain is not an island. That England (the part) is not Britain (the whole). That 'Great Britain' refers to England, Scotland, and Wales, the single kingdom created by the Treaty of Union between England and Scotland in 1707. That the 'United Kingdom' refers to the United Kingdom of Great Britain and Northern Ireland, established in 1921 and ending the 1801 union of Great Britain with Ireland (the former United Kingdom). Although the state has undergone major structural transformations since 1707, in 1801 and 1921, the catch-all term 'British' that was invented in the 18th century has endured. It may be a word in search of a definition, but in its imprecision it has also been characteristically British. As George Orwell observed, 'we call our islands by no less than six different names'. The Britishness of British politics comes laden with ambiguities. These have recently had to be confronted as devolution has unpacked one version of the United Kingdom and replaced it with another, but old habits nevertheless die hard.

Old habits are also the product of long experience. The identification of ambiguities and confusions in the British political experience should not be allowed to obscure those distinctive features which have given the political system its underlying shape and form. Many of these are buried deep in history, geography, culture, and social structure. The question of what causes what (for example, is Britain's long history of political stability a product of its political system or is its stable political system a product of a unified society and an uninterrupted history?) is endlessly asked and perennially unanswered. The truth is that everything connects with everything else, shaping and being shaped in turn. How could it be otherwise? Fortunately, this need not detain us unduly here, except as a preface to logging some of the indispensable shaping factors in the making of British politics.

Many of these are well rehearsed and require little further embellishment. However, this does not diminish their significance, or their continuing impact. The fact of geography that separated Britain from the continental land mass of Europe meant that it was unlikely to be a 'normal' European power. It has had no experience of successful invasion or occupation in its modern history (although this national story conveniently overlooked the fact that Scotland and Wales had been invaded and occupied by the English). When the countries of Europe emerged from the Second World War with the belief that the nation state had failed, requiring new pan-European political institutions to be built, Britain believed instead that it had triumphed. It was the nation's 'finest hour', when Britain had 'stood alone'.

It is impossible to understand the subsequent history of Britain's troubled relationship with 'Europe' without also understanding the force of these different historical (and geographical) trajectories. It helps to explains why Euroscepticism has been much stronger in Britain than in the rest of the EU; why Britain acquired its 'awkward partner' status; and why the 2016 referendum on EU membership produced a narrow majority to leave. In her Florence speech (in September 2017) prime minister Teresa May observed that the British have 'never totally felt at home being in the European Union', adding that 'perhaps because of our history and geography, the European Union has never felt to us like an integral part of our national story in the way it does to so many elsewhere in Europe'. However, if carried too far, this feeds a narrative of British exceptionalism which ignores the country's actual history, which included a close engagement with its continent and a developing acceptance—at least until recently—that its post-imperial future required membership of the European Common Market.

Britain avoided other major ruptures, too; or at least got them out of the way early enough to permit several centuries of orderly political evolution and continuity. Britain knew all about religious strife and struggles over the control of the state, but believed that these had largely been settled by the end of the 17th century. In the modern period (since the French Revolution), although Britain has also felt the force of the battles over nationhood, rights, freedom, democracy, and class that have shaped the modern history of Europe, it avoided an experience of decisive rupture. Without a modern revolutionary moment, Britain was not compelled to remake its political institutions, draw up a new constitution, or decide what kind of state it wanted to be. It just went on being what it was, more or less. This might be seen as a peculiar blessing, or as a kind of curse, but it is a fundamental fact about British politics.

This is usually described in the language of adaptation and flexibility (on which more will be said in Chapter 2, on the constitution). It has also been described, less pompously, as Muddling Through or (by Peter Hennessy) as the politics of a Back-of-the-Envelope nation. It is reflected in the visible continuity of the institutional landscape, still in the 21st century with a monarchy and a House of Lords, and in the predilection for not abolishing anything if it can be induced to mutate and evolve. New bits may be added on, but old bits are rarely taken away. This is why British politics *looks* so familiar, anchored in the familiar landscape of Westminster and Whitehall. Even when the reality has changed, the outward appearance of British politics looks reassuringly the same. Yet profound changes can be obscured by this appearance of continuity, raising questions about whether it is still possible to write about 'British politics' at all.

It is always difficult to judge, at any single moment, whether a political tradition is changing its underlying character as a consequence of particular events or altered circumstances, or whether its broad continuities are still intact. British politics have regularly been described by commentators over the years as being 'in transition'. It is a question much discussed again now; and for good reason. Constitutional changes are making their impact felt, along with significant shifts in Britain's society, economy, and culture. A succession of recent crises—in parliament, in finance, and in the media—have rocked institutions and damaged trust. As the political journalist Steve Richards has written, under a headline of The Great Disruption, 'ever since the 2008 financial crash UK politics has been wild and unruly' (*Prospect*, July 2017).

What seemed like aberrations have in fact been part of a recent pattern. Elections have failed to produce majorities; a peacetime coalition has been formed; parties have been convulsed by division and leadership struggles; election outcomes have confounded expectations; a nationalist party has established its dominance in Scotland, producing an independence referendum that threatened the break-up of the United Kingdom; and another nationalist party made sufficient inroads in the rest of Britain to produce a referendum that had the seismic effect of voting to take Britain out of the European Union and convulsing the political system along the way. The unexpected has become the normal. Britain is no longer exempt from the kind of political turbulence sweeping across Europe and the United States, fed by the same kind of forces. Fifty years ago it could be confidently asserted, as it was by A. H. Birch in his classic *Representative and Responsible Government* (1964), that 'there has been no support in this country for the Populist doctrine that representation is an inferior alternative to direct democracy', yet Britain has now felt the grip of a populism that is a feature of politics in all the advanced liberal democracies. We shall have to return to what all this means for British politics in Chapter 7. One thing is certain: it is much easier to identify what the 'Britishness' of British politics has consisted of in the past (for example, the militant Protestantism of the 18th century, and the imperial ideology of the 19th and early 20th centuries) than what it might consist of now or in the future.

For example, an old examination question on British politics courses used to ask students to discuss Balfour's remark that in Britain 'our whole political machinery presupposes a people so fundamentally at one that they can safely afford to bicker'. This seemed to be a truism about the British political culture, an expression of a fundamental unity that transcended differences and so enabled the political system to achieve a stable continuity despite the sharp antagonisms of party, class, and ideology. Of course, it was never quite as simple as that, but it does nevertheless identify a crucial feature of the British political experience. It was captured in an article on the meaning of the Queen's coronation in 1953 by the sociologists Shils and Young, who wrote: 'Over the past century, British society, despite distinctions of nationality and social status, has achieved a degree of moral unity equalled by no other large national state.'

The distance between then and now, when division and fragmentation seem to be the hallmark of contemporary Britain, could not be more striking. Balfour's remark might be recast as: 'a people so fundamentally divided that they can do nothing but bicker'. Of course Britain (and England in particular) was exceptionally marked by its class divisions. This defined much of its culture and manners ('The English were the only European people who sorted themselves out by class at mealtimes', observed the historian A. J. P. Taylor: 'the masses took their principal meal at midday, their betters in the evening'), and for most of the 20th century it was class that provided the foundation of political allegiance and of the political battle. But Britain was nevertheless marked by the extent of its overarching social unity. Reform, not revolution, was the watchword. Parliament, not the barricades, was the route of advance.

This unity was helped for a long period by the empire, a profoundly 'British' experience in which all could share. It brought the separate nations and classes of Britain under its generous wing, as people learnt to paint the world pink. That is why the retreat from empire—memorably captured in US Secretary of State Dean Acheson's remark in 1962 that 'Great Britain has lost an Empire and has not yet found a role'—produced prolonged policy agonizing about the country's place in the world (which continues today and has been intensified by the referendum decision to leave the European Union). The common experience of war, especially the two great conflicts of the 20th century, further strengthened social unity. It was also helped by the particular nature of the demand for welfare and social justice, which framed itself in class rather than territorial terms, forged a civic ideology of social citizenship, looked for 'British' solutions of the kind exemplified by the 'national' health service and the welfare state, and found in the British Labour Party a political instrument that gave it a local idiom and integrated it into established constitutional procedures and institutions. At the same time the BBC, as a core British institution, anchored the British in a common national conversation. This is a bald summary of a rich history, but it is an indispensable part of any understanding of British politics. If Britishness has now fragmented, it is important to understand what it has fragmented from.

It is not that Britain has lacked differences. These remain sharp and marked—of class, ethnicity, culture, generation, place, nation, religion, and much else—and some grow sharper; new issues appear as old ones subside; and traditional attitudes (such as deference, trust, and duty) are replaced by a sceptical questioning of authority and even a willingness to kick over the traces at times.

In the 1975 referendum on EU membership most people deferred to elite opinion on the matter; in the 2016 referendum elite opinion was expressly repudiated. The fragmentation of a traditional class structure has brought with it a political fragmentation. All this demands caution in making generalizations. Yet it has undoubtedly been the case that the commonality of British society has given a particular character to its politics in the past. It has not been necessary (at least not until recently, and always with Northern Ireland as the standing exception) to structure political life around religious, ethnic, or territorial divisions, or competing cultural identities, as it has often been necessary to do elsewhere. Nor has there been the regionalization of political life that is common in much of Europe. In Britain all political roads have traditionally led to London (at least since the union with Scotland), where power has been centralized and concentrated. The political conversation has been a national one. This kind of commonality is now breaking down; and a more differentiated society is already having important consequences for the political system.

The old building blocks of Britishness may now be weakening (and in need of replacement or reinvention). The legacy of empire has produced a population that is much more diverse and multicultural, raising questions about the contemporary meaning of Britishness, while immigration of all kinds has become a potent and often toxic political issue. At the same time, devolution has strengthened separate identities and threatened to break Britain up, with Scotland leading the way. This is why, as prime minister, Gordon Brown launched a campaign to promote 'British values', a campaign doomed from the start. Against this uncertain background, the popular celebration of the Queen's Diamond Jubilee in 2012, followed by the London Olympics of that year with an opening ceremony that was a hymn to Britain, could feel to many like a reaffirmation of a Britishness that had become much less sure of itself than it had been sixty years earlier.

'Suddenly we're all Britons again,' proclaimed the writer Robert McCrum (*Observer*, 19 August 2012).

Yet it was to prove a transient moment. Only four years later the EU referendum revealed a Britain that was divided against itself. There was a chasm of values, beliefs, and identities on display as Leavers and Remainers lined up against each other. The glue of a unifying Britishness seemed to have dissolved into competing versions and alternative identities. Scotland held an independence referendum. This fracturing threatened the idea of a capacious Britishness in which everyone could find a home. For example, a poll during the EU referendum found that 80 per cent of people who defined themselves as 'English' voted to leave, while 80 per cent of those who called themselves 'British' voted to remain.

Divisions of class seemed to have been replaced by divisions of age, along with divisions of education and place. The kind of Britain that felt at ease with the modern world found itself at odds with the kind of Britain that felt unsettled and left behind by economic and social change. For many people, especially those of an older generation, the loss of traditional anchorage points in their lives produced a nostalgic protest at the way the country had gone. The question of Britain's membership of the EU had unleashed a culture war. Just as British politics had once been seen as the beneficiary of a people that was fundamentally united, it had now become the battleground of a people that was deeply divided. There was no longer any agreement on the kind of country Britain was, or wanted to be.

But that is to run ahead. Speculation about where British politics might be going has to wait until we have established where it has come from, and how its essential character has been formed. What is this essential character? It has been distinguished by a striking simplicity. This can be a shock to the system for those accustomed to more elaborately ordered political arrangements elsewhere. Raymond Seitz, a former American ambassador to

Britain, describes (in his *Over Here*) what it was like to leave the tortuous legislative process of Washington and arrive in the brutal simplicities of Westminster:

> Coming from this kind of fractured, fractious federal background, an American arrives on British shores astonished to discover how unfettered a modern British government is. When I first lived here, in the mid-1970s, it took me a long time to understand that a British government, with a simple majority in the House of Commons, can do pretty much what it wants to. If the party in power can count on having one more warm body in its lobby than all the other bodies combined in the other lobby, there is nothing to prevent the government having its way. I kept looking for constitutional checks and institutional balances that could stay the will of a British government. But I could find none. In face of such arbitrary omnipotence, I could suddenly imagine myself as an American revolutionary, grabbing my flintlock from the wall above the fireplace and rushing into the forest to take a few potshots at the Redcoats.

This is often described as the British tradition of 'strong government'. It is said to reflect both a particular history and the temper of a people. It was forged out of a state that had early on established a centralized grip on its territory, earlier and tighter than elsewhere. Even though monarchs had to learn to govern with the 'consent' of representatives, eventually having to settle for a Crown-in-Parliament arrangement that concealed a fundamental shift in the balance of power in practice if not in theory, what remained intact was a governing tradition. The identity of those doing the governing may have altered, but the activity of governing remained remarkably unchanged. The arrival of democratic politics did little to disturb this tradition, perhaps even strengthening it by endowing it with an enhanced legitimacy. It was a governing arrangement that was top-down rather than bottom-up. Power was centralized and concentrated. It enabled governments to govern, or so it was said.

It was also a very British arrangement, in its governing simplicity. Government was a craft, not an artefact. It required not elaborate books of rules but an adherence to conventions and a proper apprenticeship. It could be entrusted to good chaps who could be relied upon to play the game. There need be no nonsense about the sovereignty of the people or the fundamental rights of citizens. The rule of law, grounded in the common law tradition and the independence of the judiciary, was the protector of liberty. A doctrine of representation was developed which guaranteed a safe distance between the governors and the governed. The governed seemed content to be governed in this way, as long as they had the periodic opportunity to kick one lot of governors out and put another lot in. Those who ran the state, whether as politicians, administrators, policemen, or judges, were not regarded as corrupt (as it was said of Sir Hector Rose, the Permanent Secretary in C. P. Snow's novel *The New Men*, 'it was absurd to suppose that Rose could be bought by any money under Heaven: it would be like trying to slip Robespierre a five-pound note') and it was therefore reasonable to let them get on with it.

If pushed too far such a portrait becomes a caricature, while some of its features are clearly changing. Yet it does still capture much of the essential character of the British political tradition. This is why it is necessary to add some qualifications to those descriptions of the stable, representative democracy of the 'British model' that were cited at the beginning of this chapter. To many Britain has seemed a funny, and reluctant, kind of democracy. It did not have its 4 July or 14 July moment, or nourish a culture of citizenship. David Marquand calls it 'the Strange Career of British Democracy', with competing narratives and understandings.

There had been suspicion, and fear, among the old governing classes about what democracy might bring with it, as the untutored masses staked their political claims, and much relief as it was safely domesticated by established governing traditions. It did not achieve the wholesale reorganization of the political system on democratic first principles, nor did it circumscribe those who governed with a new set of democratic accountabilities. Rather, political life went on pretty much as before. When Lord John Russell had steered the Great Reform Act of 1832 through parliament, often seen as the British alternative to continental revolution, he dismissed fears about the arrival of democracy and 'denied altogether that the measure would have the effect of rendering the House a democratic assemblage in that sense of the word'. The sense of the word he was evoking was pejorative, with democracy seen as the dangerous rule of the untutored masses. As prime minister Stanley Baldwin noted in 1928: 'Democracy has arrived at a gallop in England and I feel all the time that it is a race for life; can we educate them before the crash comes?'

What remained intact, above all else, was a strong executive centre. This was further strengthened, rather than constrained, by the arrival of democratic politics, as majority parties claimed their right to the full resources of the state without hindrance or interference. As the state grew in size and scope, a governing tradition that secured unhindered enjoyment of it was a very considerable asset indeed. All that was needed to receive its blessings was a parliamentary majority. Once in secure possession of this, the governing landscape was remarkably free of institutional blockages or impediments. There was no separation of powers to create alternative centres of authority. There were no meddling judges to tell you that what you were doing was unconstitutional. There was no constitutional rule-book to define the parameters of your power. The doctrine of parliamentary sovereignty armed you against power-sharing. You could, in short, do what you could get away with. In the language of political science: 'The Westminster system, which evolved in the years following the Glorious Revolution, is one of the most decisive in the democratic world because, in its pure form, it creates a much smaller number of veto players' (Francis Fukuyama).

It is no wonder, then, that foreign observers have been struck by the governing simplicities of the British system, or that foreign politicians have often salivated at the governing resources available to their British counterparts. A British prime minister, at least one with a united party and a secure parliamentary majority, is a far more powerful figure than an American president. Yet this governing capacity has come at a price in terms of accountability. It is a price that the British people, at least until quite recently, have seemed more than willing to pay. The journalist Hugo Young once put it like this:

> Contrary to popular myth, and to the incantations of political leaders who can hardly afford to give the question serious study, the British do not passionately care about democracy. As long as they get a vote every few years and the children don't starve, they are prepared to put up with almost anything politicians throw at them. They do not have the habit of making life difficult for government, especially a strong government. They are prepared to be quiet accessories to mandates they never really gave. This preference, which is for strong government over accountable government, is to be found throughout the British parliamentary system.
>
> (*Guardian*, 15 September 1988)

We shall have to consider whether it is still possible, in the early part of the 21st century—with stronger accountabilities, new constraints, powers devolved, disappearing majorities, populist revolt—to characterize British politics in this way. People certainly seem to have acquired the habit of making life difficult for government, never more so than in the 2016 EU referendum which had the character of a democratic uprising. A political system known for its governing strength had become distinguished by its governing weakness. Much is certainly changing, even if much also stays the same. What had certainly changed was the way in which foreign observers viewed the British. The effect of the protracted Brexit saga has been that

Britain was no longer seen as the exemplar of stable, representative government, although this may change again after a government with a secure majority was formed after the 2019 election. Whatever else Brexit had done, it had damaged how British government was viewed. The London correspondent of the *New York Times* put it like this: 'Britain—renowned for its pragmatism, its common sense, its political stability—has become nearly unrecognizable to its European allies' ('No One Knows What Britain Is Anymore', 19 November 2017). Its political skills seemed to have deserted it, along with any realism about its place in the world. British exceptionalism may have reasserted itself, but at considerable cost to its reputation for good government.

Chapter 2
The constitution: old and new

In the wake of the tensions generated by Enoch Powell's notorious 'Rivers of Blood' speech on immigration in 1968, the Labour politician and Cabinet minister Richard Crossman made this entry in his diary: 'The British constitution is like a rock against which the wave of popular emotion breaks, and one hopes that after a time the tide will go down and the rock stand untouched. This is the strength of our system, that, although in one sense we have plebiscitary democracy, actually the leadership is insulated from the masses by the existence of parliament. Parliament is the buffer which enables our leadership to avoid saying yes or no to the electorate in the hope that, given time, the situation can be eased away' (27 April 1968). Fifty years on, things feel very different. The constitutional rock has been pounded from all sides and has seemed near to breaking point.

But that is to run ahead. The first task is to establish what this 'British constitution' is. The British do not know very much about constitutions, at least in the sense that they are known about elsewhere. They are not even familiar with the basic language of constitutional debate and seem resolutely indifferent to constitutional issues. They enjoy the kind of constitutional illiteracy that comes from a particular political history. This is not because they have no constitution (as has often been alleged), but because they have had a constitution of a peculiar kind. Above all else it has been a political rather than legal constitution, shaped and reshaped by changing political circumstances and so forever on the move. This makes it peculiarly difficult to pin down. Some regard this as a grave disability, others as a rich blessing.

Constitutions are rules of the political game, or at least the most important ones. They tell you how the game should be played. Usually there is a book of rules, as in other games, so that it is easy to check whether the game is being played properly. This also provides something to wave in the face of cheats. Yet it may impose a straitjacket too, preventing the game's natural evolution and development in response to new players and changed circumstances. Further, even where there is a book of rules, it may not accurately describe how the game is actually played. Britain is rare among democratic states (only Israel and New Zealand belong to the same category) in not having a codified book of constitutional rules. There are lots of rules that are written down, though, from ancient statutes such as the Bill of Rights of 1689 and the Act of Settlement of 1701 to very recent legislation on human rights, devolution, freedom of information, party funding, and fixed-term parliaments. If all this constitutional legislation was brought together, it would make a vast and impressive volume. Indeed, following the 2010 general election, some of it was brought together by the Cabinet Secretary in *The Cabinet Manual*, described as 'a guide to laws, conventions and rules on the operation of government'.

This is why it has always been misleading to describe Britain as having an unwritten constitution, or no proper constitution at all. Rather it has a constitution that is not codified or enacted into a single book of rules. It is a great accumulated jumble of statutes, common law provisions and precedents, conventions and guidebooks. As such it is an awesome mess, horrifying to constitutional purists but an authentic expression of a particular history. It is a political constitution, but also a historical one. The constitutional shed is crammed full of all the objects collected over a long political lifetime. Nobody is quite sure which still work, or whether some have been superseded by others, even as more objects are squeezed in. From time to time someone (a Bagehot or a Dicey) tries to describe the contents in a coherent and intelligible way, although this description may differ somewhat from the last time it was attempted. Occasionally it is suggested (most recently by Gordon Brown, prime minister from 2007 to 2010, who floated the idea of a written constitution) that the shed should be sorted out once and for all, and everything put into a proper order, but this has always seemed a much too daunting task and the need has never been sufficiently pressing. If more room was needed, then it was easier just to add on an extension.

The vindication of such arrangements, or so it was traditionally argued, was that they worked. 'We Englishmen are Very Proud of our Constitution, Sir', declared Dickens's Mr Podsnap: 'It was Bestowed Upon Us by Providence. No Other Country is so Favoured as This Country.' In its combination of liberty with order, and in its protections against arbitrary government, the British constitution seemed to offer lessons to the world. Certainly this was widely believed in the 18th century, as the 'matchless constitution' that had been bequeathed by the Glorious Revolution of 1688 was celebrated at home and admired from abroad. Parliament had disciplined royal power, the independence of judges had been safeguarded, and the resulting system of intrinsic checks and balances could be presented as the exemplar of a proper constitutionalism. The 'true excellence' of this form of government, according to Blackstone's *Commentaries on the Laws of England* (1765-9), was that 'all the parts of it form a mutual check upon each other'.

The idea of balance was held to be fundamental, producing a practical form of 'mixed' government that prevented tyranny while enabling effectiveness. The growing dominance of the Commons was balanced by the influence of the Crown and the Lords, thus securing a constitutional equilibrium. 'It is by this mixture of monarchical, aristocratical and democratic power, blended together in one system, and by these three estates balancing one another, that our free constitution has been preserved so long inviolate,' declared another 18th-century constitutional theorist, Henry St John Bolingbroke, adding: 'It secures society against the miseries which are inseparable from simple forms of government, and is as liable as little as possible to the inconveniences that arise in mixed forms.' Alongside these ideas of balance and mixture was the concept of a separation of powers (between executive, legislative, and judicial functions) as an axial constitutional principle. In his *The Spirit of the Laws* (1748), Montesquieu famously translated what he believed to be the model of such an admirable and ingenious separation in Britain into a more general constitutional formula that was to be influential with those (like the American founding fathers) seeking to construct constitutions on the basis of sound principles.

There is a good deal of irony in all of this, since the British system has since come to be characterized as peculiarly lacking in institutional checks and balances and with the principle of a separation of powers conspicuous by its absence, at least in any pure form. These were really no more than descriptions and interpretations of a historical constitution at certain moments in its development, heavily influenced in many cases by the political predilections of the commentators themselves, rather than accounts of securely anchored constitutional principles. Yet they have been, and remain, influential in shaping beliefs about the constitution. The traditional notion of a constitutional balance between Crown, Lords, and Commons is still captured by the reference to the 'Crown-in-Parliament' as the formal source of legislative authority. Even today every law passed by parliament begins with these words: 'Be it enacted by the Queen's most Excellent Majesty, by and with the advice and consent of the Lords Spiritual and Temporal, and Commons, in this present Parliament assembled, and by the authority of the same...'

Note how 'and Commons' just sneaks in to this august assemblage. This is the moment to summon up the ghost of Walter Bagehot, whose celebrated account of *The English Constitution* (1867) sought to strip away the appearance from the reality, the 'dignified' from the 'efficient'. Like so many anxious 19th-century minds, Bagehot wanted to know how the pressures from an advancing democracy could be contained within the parameters of an ancient constitution. He found the answer in an elaborate system of smoke and mirrors. The 'dignified' constitution (in which the monarchy played a crucial role) would continue to provide a focus for the 'vacant many', while the 'efficient' constitution passed into the hands of a middle-class House of Commons and the Cabinet ('a combining committee—a hyphen which joins, a buckle which fastens, the legislative part of the State to the executive part of the State') now provided the mechanism to keep the governing show on the road. It was a striking portrait, with the efficient secret of the constitution no longer located in the separation of powers but in their fusion. The nature of the governing mixture had changed.

Yet there remained a real conundrum once traditional accounts of a balanced constitution were abandoned, as they had to be once the dominance of the Commons was underwritten by an advancing democracy. The conundrum turned on the principle of parliamentary sovereignty, long enshrined as the organizing principle of legislative authority in Britain, and how it could be reconciled with an old system of checks and balances once power was fused and a parliamentary majority could deploy it to secure its unhindered way. If parliamentary sovereignty meant that parliament could do anything it liked, and if this sovereignty was now effectively exercised by the Commons alone (once the 1911 Parliament Act had put the Lords in its place), and if the Commons was now in the iron grip of the executive (courtesy of the rigid party system), where did this leave the constitution? Where were the checks and balances? Where was the protection against arbitrary government? Where were the limits of the state?

Such questions have become central to modern constitutional (and political) argument in Britain, but they were already surfacing at the end of the 19th century when A. V. Dicey's classic interpretation of the constitution appeared (*Introduction to the Study of the Law of the Constitution*, 1885). This is relevant here, since its purpose was to navigate an old constitution into a new democratic legitimacy. If the sovereignty of parliament ('the right to make or unmake any law whatever') was the 'one fundamental law of the British Constitution', how was this to be reconciled with the fundamental democratic principle of the sovereign people? What was there to prevent a sovereign parliament exercising arbitrary power over a sovereign people?

These were Dicey's questions, just as they remain ours. His answer rejected any resort to the formal rigidities of constitutions elsewhere, which were inferior in every respect to 'the most flexible polity in existence', anchored in the rule of law and conventional understandings. The reason why the legal sovereignty of parliament could not in practice lead to arbitrary government, despite the theoretical possibility, was that it was now firmly rooted in the political sovereignty of the electorate. A parliamentary majority would only do what a majority of the people wanted. Legal sovereignty and political sovereignty went hand in hand, such that 'our modern code of constitutional morality secures, though in a roundabout way, what is called abroad the "sovereignty of the people"'. The circle was squared, and the constitution had been safely navigated—without the need for radical overhaul—into new democratic waters.

But had it really? Even Dicey came to doubt it, once he switched role from academic jurist to Liberal Unionist partisan. In the former role he demonstrated why a sovereign parliament would always serve the wishes of a sovereign people; in the latter role he denounced it for failing to do so. This Dicey wanted to know how a transient Commons majority could 'arrogate to itself that legislative omnipotence which of right belongs to the nation' and warned (the context was the 1911 Parliament Act) that 'no country, except England, now dreams of placing itself under the rule of a single elected House'. He therefore looked to the referendum as a protective constitutional device ('a democratic check on democratic evils') against the misuse of parliamentary sovereignty by temporary majorities. It is not necessary to share Dicey's politics, or to agree with his remedy, to think that he was on to something.

These sorts of arguments were not to be heard again until much later in the 20th century, after a long period of intervening calm on the constitutional front. The 20th century was the era when disciplined party government really came into its own, with its legitimizing armoury of mandates and manifestos, and a constitution which enabled a majority party to deploy parliamentary sovereignty without check or hindrance proved especially congenial to its governing purposes. The idea that the legal sovereignty of parliament merely reflected the political sovereignty of the people, and that this was the end of the argument as far as democracy was concerned, was a brutally simple and compelling constitutional perspective. It really required no further discussion, and for a long period received none.

What it produced (and justified) was a constitution in which power was highly concentrated, where the prerogatives of the Crown had become the powers of the executive, and where formal constraints on that power were notable by their absence. Behind the constitutional doctrine of parliamentary sovereignty was the political reality of executive sovereignty. In international terms, Britain was out on a limb. There was no book of constitutional rules; no supreme court to guard the constitution against the politicians; no charter of citizens' rights that had to be complied with; no other tiers of government that enjoyed constitutional status and protection; no second chamber with power to rival the first; and no electoral system that enforced proportionality between votes cast and seats won. This was a 'winner-takes-all' system with a vengeance, not just in terms of how the first-past-the-post electoral system worked but in terms of the governing resources available to a winning party. Getting your hands on the great prize of government, with all its unconstrained power, conditioned everything. The style and culture of political life, with its embedded adversarialism, both reflected and reinforced the essential nature of this system.

It was a system in which it was difficult to say what was 'unconstitutional' at any particular moment, or by whom this could be said with any authority (as became clear in the arguments around Brexit). It was also a system in which 'constitutional' laws had no special status or recognition, and were not subject to any separate procedure in their making, unmaking, or amending. When the House of Commons passes a piece of constitutional legislation it does not identify it as such or apply distinctive procedures to its consideration or extra conditions to its approval. Constitutional laws are simply ordinary laws with a constitutional subject matter. Nor can they be entrenched in any formal way, since a sovereign parliament can make or unmake any law whatsoever, including laws about the constitution. Such laws (for example, the 2011 Fixed-term Parliaments Act, which the Johnson government elected in 2019 wants to repeal) will endure for as long as they are politically acceptable, not because they enjoy any special or protected status. This is also why, far more than the absence of a codified book of rules, Britain has sometimes been thought not to have a constitution at all.

The 'constitutional' laws passed in the early part of the 20th century had set the framework for political life for fifty years afterwards, without any serious challenge or controversy. The ascendancy of the Commons over the Lords, and therefore of the executive over the political system, had been finally established in the 1911 Parliament Act (with a further tightening in 1949). Universal suffrage was finally achieved in the 1918 Representation of the People Act, though all women over 21 were not included until 1928. That Britain would remain a unitary state seemed finally established when the prospect of Home Rule for Ireland leading to a quasi-federal 'home rule all round' ended with the 1921 Anglo-Irish Treaty. This represented a spectacular failure of constitutional politics in Britain, neither keeping Ireland in the union nor freeing it completely from it, but it was nevertheless a settlement of a kind.

These measures served to keep the constitution off the political agenda for a large part of the 20th century. Then it began to creep back in, from a number of different directions, until by the end of the century Britain found itself in the thick of a constitutional revolution. What had happened to bring this about? The biggest jolt to the traditional constitution was the one that was least noticed at the time. When Britain joined the Common Market (now European Union) in 1972, it may have believed that it was simply joining an economic club but in fact it was transforming its constitution. In giving primacy to European law over domestic law in the ever-expanding areas where EU law held sway (a position confirmed in pivotal legal judgements in Britain), the old doctrine of parliamentary sovereignty was effectively blown out of the water. Parliament was no longer sovereign, except in the formal sense that it could still vote to leave the European Union if it wanted to (which is exactly what happened in the 2016 referendum).

There was much bewilderment, and gnashing of political teeth, in Britain as it was slowly realized what had been done. There were claims that when the British people had voted to confirm the country's membership of 'Europe' in a referendum in 1975, they had been innocent of the constitutional enormity of their decision (and deliberately kept so, in some versions). This produced much railing against 'rule by Brussels' and ensured that the European issue rumbled away in the interstices of British politics, periodically exploding, especially in the Conservative Party. When it culminated in a new referendum, and a decision to leave the EU, this unleashed a constitutional crisis that rocked the political system.

Before exploring this further, though, note should be taken of other developments that were unsettling a constitutional settlement that had for long remained uncontested. The sharper ideological antagonisms of the 1970s and 1980s had thrown into relief the nature of a political system which delivered such unconstrained power to parties which enjoyed diminishing levels of electoral support. When the Conservative politician Lord Hailsham, with Labour in his sights, coined the phrase 'elective dictatorship' in the 1970s to describe the contemporary constitution, it found a wide resonance. Many thought that the term received its practical demonstration in the Conservative governments of Mrs Thatcher after 1979, which seemed to display a 'one of us' governing arrogance and barely concealed contempt for the conventional rules of the game. This period served to provide a crash course of constitutional education and helped to promote new attention to issues of constitutional reform.

More immediate pressures came from the growing demand in Scotland (and also, less so, in Wales) for serious devolution of power. The need to respond to this pressure produced an abortive Royal Commission on the Constitution in the 1970s and devolution referendums in Scotland and Wales, but twenty years later the pressure was even more intense and could no longer be safely contained by the centre. If the union was to be preserved, it clearly had to be reformed. Then, as ever, there was Northern Ireland, which became a constant preoccupation for British governments (if not for the British people, who adopted a despairingly blind eye to the province) once the post-1921 version of self-government broke down and direct rule was reimposed in 1972, requiring endless initiatives in constitutional ingenuity in an effort to find a way of governing that divided community.

What all this meant was that, in the final quarter of the 20th century, the constitution was on the move again. New political pressures (including an atmosphere of sleaze and distrust) were demanding a response. A famously flexible constitution was about to be stretched to the limit, perhaps even beyond. The decisive moment came with the election of Tony Blair's Labour government in 1997, with its commitment to a range of sweeping constitutional reforms. For the first time in Britain's modern history the process of constitutional change and adaptation was not to occur merely as a response to events and pressures, but as a deliberately engineered programme of constitutional revolution (Figure 2). As Blair himself had put it in 1996:

> Changing the way we govern, and not just changing our government is no longer an optional extra for Britain.... Times have changed. Constitutional issues are now at the heart of political debate. We gauge that constitutional conservatism is dying and that popular support for change is tangible and steadfast.

The constitution would never be the same again, nor intended to be.

The sheer scale of the reform programme was extraordinary, as was the extent to which it was actually delivered and the speed with which this was done. Two measures stand out. The devolution of power to Scotland (vast) and Wales (limited) represented a fundamental break with a traditionally centralized and unitary state. It created new political systems and new political cultures. Then the Human Rights Act (1998), effectively incorporating the European Convention on Human Rights into domestic law, introduced a new judicial benchmark against which actions of public authorities (and Acts of Parliament) have to be tested. Although it did not involve a full-blown constitutional court, nor a power for judges to strike down Acts of Parliament, there is no doubt that the 1998 Human Rights Act has to be set alongside the 1972 European Communities Act in putting a new constitutional framework around British politics.

2. **Reforming the machine** (*Economist*, 18 April 1998).

On all sides the impact of change and reform was felt. Most hereditary peers were removed from the House of Lords and further reform was promised. Northern Ireland acquired an Assembly that, in its composition and operation, was a triumph of constitutional ingenuity. London acquired a new local authority, with a directly elected mayor. An official inquiry considered and recommended a new voting system for Westminster. Freedom of information legislation challenged a traditional secrecy. Party funding and electoral organization became the province of a new Electoral Commission, which joined an expanding set of constitutional watchdogs. Control over interest rates, and therefore over monetary policy, was transferred from the Treasury to the Monetary Policy Committee of the Bank of England, thus creating a new and independent source of power within the government of Britain. The visible separation of power was strengthened as judges moved from the House of Lords into a new Supreme Court. New kinds of electoral systems sprouted all over the place (except at Westminster) and referendums became the established vehicles for approving constitutional change.

Merely to recite such a catalogue of reform between 1997 and 2010 is enough to register its significance for British politics. It made it possible, and plausible, to announce (as did Anthony King, in his 2001 Hamlyn Lectures *Does the United Kingdom Still have a Constitution?*) that 'the traditional British constitution . . . is dead'. If so, it was not clear what kind of new constitution had been born. Much had changed, but much had also stayed the same. There may have been a constitutional revolution, but there had been no grand design behind it and no concerted attempt to make its constituent elements fit together into a coherent whole. Yet it had unleashed a constitutional dynamic that would bring enduring (and unpredictable) consequences for British politics.

One consequence was a developing tension between politicians and judges, notably on the matter of human rights. There seemed to be a conflict between two constitutional principles: the sovereignty of parliament and the rule of law. Who should decide—the judges or the politicians? As Tom Bingham, who had been the country's top judge, observed in his luminous *The Rule of Law*: 'Our constitutional settlement has become unbalanced, and the power to restrain legislation favoured by a clear majority in the Commons has become much weakened, even if, exceptionally such legislation were to infringe the rule of law.' A way had to be found to manage the potential for tension in the new relationship. Judges had become players in British politics in a way that they had formerly not been.

A further consequence of constitutional change was the momentum it gave to the process of devolution. This had been designed to preserve the union; but it now threatened to destroy it. In 2011 the Nationalists moved from minority to majority rule in Scotland and this enabled them in 2014 to hold a referendum on Scottish independence. Independence was rejected, but the issue was not settled (with Brexit reactivating it) and the future of the British state itself was now in question. It opened up debate about identities and loyalties of a kind that Britain had not experienced in its modern history. Even the English started asking questions about their own identity and how it might find political expression. It was no longer certain that Britain would continue to exist; and if it did it would be very different from the unitary state of old.

Even after Labour's constitutional revolution, the coalition government that followed had constitutional ambitions of its own. Liberal Democrat leader Nick Clegg, now deputy prime minister, even promised the biggest reform of British democracy 'since 1832'. In the event a referendum on changing the electoral system to the Alternative Vote was decisively lost in 2011; and another proposal to reform the House of Lords by introducing elections was undermined by Conservative opposition and met the fate of similar proposals made under the previous Labour government. However legislation on fixed-term parliaments was introduced, significantly restricting the power of dissolution (though not preventing Teresa May holding a surprise election in 2017, only two years after the previous one, nor Boris Johnson calling another election in 2019).

But it was the referendum vote to leave the EU that delivered the real constitutional bombshell. If joining the EU had been a pivotal constitutional moment, then leaving provided an even more momentous one. Henceforth laws would be made by the British parliament and given effect in British courts. However, the referendum itself raised questions about the place of referendums in British constitutional arrangements; and whether parliamentary sovereignty had now been replaced by the popular sovereignty of direct democracy. The process of giving effect to the referendum decision plunged Britain into constitutional controversy. Former prime minister Gordon Brown even described it as 'our most serious constitutional crisis since the 17th century' (*Observer*, 11 August 2019). Under Article 50 of the Treaty of European Union a state wishing to withdraw must do so 'in accordance with its own constitutional arrangements'. The problem with Britain's famously flexible constitution was that there was no agreement about what these constitutional arrangements were. The government sought to proceed by using the power of executive prerogative, but this was challenged in the courts and culminated in a Supreme Court judgement that declared: 'We cannot accept that a major change to UK constitutional arrangements can be achieved by ministers alone; it must be effected in the only way that the UK constitution recognises, namely by Parliamentary legislation.'

This put judges at the centre of the political stage. They were even denounced as 'enemies of the people' by the Brexit-supporting press. Yet all they had done was to uphold the constitutional role of parliament; and it seemed odd that those who had wanted to leave the European Union in the name of parliamentary sovereignty should have objected to this affirmation of parliament's rights. But the withdrawal process was only the beginning, difficult as it was. As the referendum decision had provided no guidance about the terms of a post-departure relationship with the EU, tortuous negotiations ensured that parliament's role would be crucial. When the Johnson government announced that parliament would be suspended (prorogued in the jargon) for an extended period, the matter was again taken to the courts. In a momentous judgement (in September 2019), the Supreme Court ruled that the suspension was unlawful and offended against the constitutional principles of parliamentary sovereignty and parliamentary accountability. In the words of the judges, 'the courts have the responsibility of upholding the values and principles of our constitution and making them effective. It is their particular responsibility to determine the legal limits of the powers conferred on each branch of government, and to decide whether any exercise of power has transgressed those limits. The courts cannot shirk that responsibility merely on the ground that the question raised is political in tone or context.'

Britain might not have a written constitution, but it had nevertheless acquired a constitutional court. The fact that much of constitutional practice depended upon conventions did not prevent the courts having a role if these conventions were breached. The exercise of executive prerogative power was constrained by limits of constitutional principle, which the courts had an obligation to enforce. There was a time when the courts, knowing their constitutional place, would have steered clear of any involvement in contentious political issues. That has now changed. The fact that Britain had an uncodified constitution made it more, not less, important that the courts should be the guardians of constitutional principles. Henceforth no account of British politics would be complete without a recognition that the judges had become major constitutional players.

The referendum might have been straightforward, but it had taken the British polity into a minefield of constitutional complexity. Had it produced a constitutional crisis? This was widely asserted, and it certainly tested a constitution that depended upon conventions to make it work, yet in many ways the crisis was more political than constitutional. There is no doubt that the tension between direct democracy and representative democracy generated a profound constitutional challenge. It also tested the relationship between government and parliament, as parliament sought to take control of the Brexit process. The position of Scotland and Northern Ireland, both of which had voted to stay in the European Union, ensured that issues of the union could not be avoided. Yet in some ways Britain's flexible constitution, with its reputation for being able to respond to whatever was thrown at it, should have been well placed to accommodate the traumas of Brexit. It was less a constitutional failure and more a failure of the party system and of the conduct of politics.

Where did all this leave the old political constitution at the end of the second decade of the 21st century? The short answer was that it was dead and buried, although it was less clear what it had been replaced by. Where there had once been such simplicity, there was now complexity. Where there had been a clear and unrestricted line of governing authority, there was now a whole array of checks and constraints. Power that had been concentrated was now divided up. What had once been decided politically was now decided by codes, rules, courts, and commissions. The sovereignty of parliament was challenged; the separation of powers enhanced. In the words of Vernon Bogdanor (in his *The New British Constitution*) this represented 'the beginning of the transformation of Britain into a constitutional state'.

It also made governing a lot more difficult. From activist judges to devolved parliaments, and from a more confident House of Lords to a less compliant House of Commons, governments had many more hurdles to get across. Brexit tested a system that relied on conventional understandings to make it work. It also revealed that the country that gave the world parliamentary government had still not established a proper constitutional relationship between executive and legislature. Governing without a secure majority had challenged the assumptions of a traditional kind of politics. Yet the 20th-century charge had been that government had become too easy and unrestrained; and that a political constitution needed to be constitutionalized. In many respects this had begun to happen, but not in any coherent way. It was all a bit of a mess, compounded by the fallout from the decision to leave the EU. Some thought it was time to sort the mess out (and write the constitution down), but too much remained uncertain and disputed for this to be a practical proposition. At a time when politicians find it hard to agree on anything, it is extremely unlikely that agreement could be found on a new constitution.

At some point events may conspire to provoke some serious constitution-making. The fallout from Brexit might have been such an event, although the Conservative government elected in 2019 wanted to use its majority to make some constitutional changes of its own. In the absence of anything more comprehensive, muddling along and tidying up is likely to continue to be the order of the day.

Chapter 3
Arguing: the politics of ideas

Politics is about power, but it is also about ideas. Much of politics can just seem like a game, its participants obsessed with tactical advantage, but behind the game there are ideas struggling to get out. Argument is the meat and drink of politics. Often this is sterile and routinized, but at issue are also different sets of ideas about the world. But these ideas do not exist in a vacuum. They become effective only when they connect with the world as it is lived, offering electorates convincing explanations and remedies for the problems they face. Politicians know this, which is why they are always trying to construct 'narratives' and to 'frame' arguments that pull policies together in a way that is designed to win the battle of ideas. Winning this battle is seen as crucial to winning power.

In Britain the nature of political argument has taken a particular form. Its political culture is one of institutionalized adversarialism. Governments govern and oppositions oppose. That is how the system works. It is how the House of Commons is structured and organized and it is how politics is conducted and reported. This gives a ritual character to much political argument. It was nicely satirized in an edition of the BBC Radio Four's *The Now Show* in 2016, with this version of a typical news programme:

Today the Government announced plans for a Thing. With me is a man implacably opposed to the Thing and a man totally in favour of the Thing.

Man in favour of the Thing: Why are you in favour? 'Well this is a marvellous Thing that will benefit the country and enrich all our lives.'

Man opposed to the Thing: What is wrong with the Thing? 'This Thing without any doubt will be the worst Thing that has ever happened to anyone anywhere and according to our research could well bring disaster upon us all.'

Well, thank you both, and I hope our viewers are now better informed.

In exaggerated form, this is exactly how much political argument in Britain has been conducted and reported (and why so many people have been turned off by it). It is instantly clear if it is a politician who is speaking. Politics ceases to be a conversation; and there is no incentive to find common ground, as demonstrated most vividly by the arguments around Brexit. The nature of the country's tabloid press has contributed to this difficulty, with its culture of simplistic vilification. Britain is not a consensus-seeking kind of democracy (of the Nordic variety) but one of organized antagonism. Some see merit in this, in clarifying alternatives, but it does give a sterile character to much political argument.

Because politics is conducted like this, it becomes harder to see the big picture. Politics needs argument, but when everything is argued about it can be difficult to distinguish real arguments from synthetic ones and significant issues from trivial ones. For their part politicians seek constantly to construct an overarching storyline (as in the vacuous 'Brexit means Brexit') with its associated 'lines to take', which compresses arguments into neat presentational packages.

All this can make it difficult to see the real battle of ideas that is taking place. Yet if a political tradition is to be understood, it is important to know what it argues about. Since the EU referendum in June 2016, argument about Brexit has dominated everything. Before discussing that though, some account is needed of the nature of traditional political argument in Britain. By listening in to Britain's continuing political argument we can discover, as with all arguments, what matters to the participants. It is only possible to hear snatches of this argument here, but enough to get a sense of what the battle of political ideas in Britain has been about—and where the battleground is now.

Let us start with our old friends 'left' and 'right'. Much of the British political argument during the past century has been framed by these terms. They have their origin in the French Revolution, and have shaped the political experience of Europe (and beyond) for much of the time since then. They have marked off reformers from reactionaries, liberals from conservatives, and socialists from capitalists. Liberals value individual liberty and limited government; conservatives emphasize traditional authority and social order. Socialists embrace collective action for social justice and the common good; capitalists espouse market freedom for enterprise and efficiency. Here, in a nutshell, is the terrain upon which much political argument in the West has been conducted for the last two centuries, in different modulations and idioms. It has been a running argument between versions of liberty, equality, and order, and between what the state (on behalf of an idea of community) should properly do and what should be left to markets and individual choices. Parties and classes have organized themselves around the ideological formulations constructed out of these arguments.

How does Britain fit into this general picture? 'The dialectic between the growing pressures of collectivism and the opposing libertarian tendency is the one supreme fact of our domestic political life as this has developed over the past century and a half': so begins a leading account of British political ideology (W. H. Greenleaf's volume on *The Ideological Heritage* (1983), part of his larger study of the British political tradition). Well, yes and no. Perhaps that is what 'dialectic' means here. Although the growth of state provision, under the pressure of democratic forces, is certainly a central fact of Britain's modern history, how this was played out in practice is more complicated and mixed up than the notion of 'opposing tendencies' suggests and reflects distinctive features of the British political tradition.

For Britain had a peculiar 'left' and a peculiar 'right'. British socialism stood outside the tradition of continental Marxism. It was reformist in method and ethical in belief, allied with a heavy dose of trade-union pragmatism. It did not threaten traditional institutions (not even the monarchy), but wanted to use them for its improving purposes. Equally, British conservatism stood outside the tradition of continental reaction. A reactionary critic once remarked that the trouble with British conservatism was that it had not put the clock back by even one minute. It was a 'dispositional' conservatism that prided itself on its lack of fixed ideological positions, had learnt from Edmund Burke about the need to reform in order to preserve, from Disraeli about the need to attend to the condition of the whole nation, and espoused a statecraft designed to keep the ship of state afloat in choppy waters. Even British liberalism stood outside continental traditions, not least in its embrace (early in the 20th century) of a 'new' liberalism that acknowledged that liberty could often be enlarged rather than diminished by collective action.

This is why it can be misleading to describe the central tension of the British political tradition as that between collectivism and libertarianism. The dominant ideological forces in 20th-century British politics, on left and right, both believed in a strong state. The socialist left wanted to enlarge and deploy the state for its collectivist purposes, while the conservative right was attached to the state as the repository of authority and tradition. The left attacked the right for its selfish defence of privilege and inequality, and the right attacked the left for its divisive class envy and levelling ambitions. Yet behind these ferocious antagonisms, which were the stuff of much of 20th-century British politics, there were some important affinities between Tory democracy and socialist collectivism. As Samuel Beer pointed out in his classic study of *Modern British Politics* (1965), 'Socialist Democracy and Tory Democracy have a great deal in common', not least the fact that they shared an outlook that 'legitimizes a massive concentration of political power'.

These affinities helped to keep British democracy afloat in troubled times. With a left that was gradualist, reformist, and constitutional, and a right that was adaptive and responsive, there was much procedural common ground. Yet it was more than merely procedural. The left wanted to reform capitalism rather than abolish it, while the right was not imprisoned by the laissez-faire inheritance of 19th-century liberalism. This enabled Harold Macmillan (later to become Conservative prime minister) to suggest in his influential *The Middle Way* (1938) that the right course of action involved 'a new synthesis of Capitalist and Socialist theory'. There were no ideological barriers to interference and intervention, on left or right. Both traditions believed in doing things to people (whether by desire or necessity) and in drawing upon the top-down inheritance of the British state for this purpose.

Yet this was the silent conversation, rooted in shared assumptions about political power. The noisy 20th-century conversation between left and right drowned it out. The left demanded social justice and equality, which the right denounced as a threat to liberty, which in turn the left described as a cloak for privilege. The left wanted planning, regulation, and ownership for the common good, while the right railed against the threat to enterprise and the perils of bureaucratic uniformity. The language of class confronted the categories of individualism. The right attacked the left for its divisive attachment to class over nation, the foreignness of its creed (for a long time routinely accompanied by references to the Soviet Union), and general lack of patriotism. The left attacked the right for wrapping itself in the flag, xenophobia, and Little Englandism.

Someone listening in to political argument in Britain at various points in the last hundred years would soon pick up these familiar cadences. What they would almost certainly miss, though, is the extent of the agreement about power and the political system. They would not hear powerful voices, on either left or right, arguing that the traditional concentration of power in Britain should be diffused and pluralized, with new centres of power and new accountabilities, or that citizenship should be reconstituted. This is nicely illustrated by a quick comparison of two post-1945 books on the political system, one from the Labour left (Harold Laski's *Reflections on the Constitution*, 1951) and one from the Tory right (Leo Amery's *Thoughts on the Constitution*, 1947). From their different ideological perspectives, both agreed that Britain's top-down, government-centred way of doing politics should be defended and protected. In Amery's Tory view, it was essentially an executive-led system, with a passive people, and it was only the liberals and radicals of the 19th century who had 'grievously misled' opinion on the fundamental historical truth that the British system was one of 'government of the people, for the people, with, but not by, the people'. Now turn to the socialist Laski, who saw the job of the people as 'the creation of a Government which can govern' and was opposed to anything (such as proportional representation or devolution) which threatened 'the stability of executive power'. Across the ideological boundary lines, here was a crucial affinity.

It was an affinity that lurked behind the noisy arguments of British politics, complicating any attempt to fit these arguments within the confines of a simple 'collectivism versus liberty' narrative. This becomes clear if we look briefly at the major

3. Attlee and Thatcher: making and unmaking the post-war settlement.

doctrinal waves which have shaped the contours of British politics from the end of the Second World War to the recent past. Three stand out. Let us personalize them by calling them the Attlee, Thatcher, and Blair revolutions. It does not matter that these individuals were not themselves innovative thinkers. What matters is that their periods of political leadership are associated with seismic shifts in the tectonic plates of British politics. In each case they rode the wave of a shifting tide of ideas. They therefore provide the point of entry into indispensable arguments.

The Attlee revolution (Clement Attlee (Figure 3a) was prime minister in the 1945–51 Labour governments) inaugurated what is often called the 'post-war settlement', which endured in its essentials for a long generation. The landslide election of Labour's first majority government in 1945, with Churchill rejected as soon as the war was won, might have felt like a revolution at the time ('I am stunned and shocked by the country's treachery', declared the Conservative MP 'Chips' Channon to his diary), but it carried over into the post-war world the social solidarity of wartime with its ethos of 'fair shares for all'. There was a general determination not to return to the poverty, inequality, and unemployment of the pre-war years, and to use all the resources of the state to win the peace just as they had been so energetically mobilized to win the war. It was the high point of British social democratic collectivism, as industries were nationalized, redistribution advanced, and the welfare state constructed. It was also sternly centralizing, in the interests of equity and uniformity, and with an expanded state as the object and agency of change. As was said at the time, it was a period when the gentlemen in Whitehall really did know best.

Even though the Attlee revolution had run out of steam by 1951, when the electorate opted again for Conservative 'freedom', it endured in its essentials for a further generation. There is room for argument about the exact extent of the doctrinal consensus between the 1950s and the 1970s, but not about its existence. The Attlee revolution was locked in. Labour constantly looked back to it with a nostalgic and reaffirming glow, uncertain about where the left should go next, disputing between its 'fundamentalists' and 'revisionists', with Crosland's *The Future of Socialism* (1956) providing the key revisionist text. The Conservatives, in an explicit act of political adjustment, had accepted the framework of economic management (for full employment), a 'mixed' economy with a substantial public sector, and the commitment to social welfare bequeathed by the Attlee revolution. This was the 'Keynes-plus-Beveridge' world of post-war British politics.

It was the collapse of this world in the 1970s that provided the opening for the Thatcher revolution (Margaret Thatcher (Figure 3b) became leader of the Conservative Party in 1975 and was prime minister from 1979 to 1990). As the post-war settlement became unsettled, under the pressures of accelerating inflation, rising unemployment, and industrial strife (culminating in the notorious 'winter of discontent' of 1978–9), a 'new' right saw its opportunity to wage an intellectual and political assault on the whole set of assumptions that had underpinned post-war British politics, on both left and right. One of Mrs Thatcher's key intellectual lieutenants, Keith Joseph, captured the nature of the moment when he declared: 'It was only in April 1974 that I was converted to Conservatism. I had thought I was a Conservative, but I now see that I was not really one at all.' It was intended to be a revolutionary moment, and so it turned out.

In a decisive break from the accommodative traditions of 'one nation' conservatism, the Thatcherite apostles of the 'new', neo-liberal conservatism set about unpicking the post-war settlement. They attacked the bloated state and rolled back its frontiers in the name of market freedom (privatizing where the Attlee revolution had nationalized); championed self-reliance and denounced dependency; disciplined the trade unions in the cause of enterprise; and junked post-war ideas about social justice and equality in favour of a creed of individual mobility and liberty. Their model was the United States; their enemy was continental Europe. Their intellectual mentors included Friedrich von Hayek, the philosopher of the reduced state, and the philosopher of monetarist economics, Milton Friedman. It was Friedman who once described Mrs Thatcher as not being a Tory at all, but really 'a nineteenth-century liberal'.

This is a revealingly inaccurate phrase. If it captures the extent to which the new conservatism was different from the old, in its embrace of 19th-century free market liberalism, it completely misses the extent to which it was ferociously anti-liberal in its attachment to (and deployment of) the unchecked power of the centralized British state. Far from wanting to circumscribe this power, the Thatcher revolution sought energetically to exploit it to snuff out any alternative centres of power (such as local government, and the trade unions). It was not detained by the conventional rules of the constitutional game, and certainly did not want to construct any new ones that could inhibit what governments could do. Critical observers coined phrases such as 'authoritarian populism' and 'free market and strong state' to describe this aspect of the Thatcher revolution, at once liberal in economics and uncompromisingly Tory in politics.

It was a potent combination, which transformed the landscape of British politics. It certainly demolished the post-war settlement (Mrs Thatcher had famously described her purpose as the abolition of 'socialism' once and for all), but whether a new settlement had been established was less clear. This was the explicit purpose, and claim, of the Blair revolution that followed (Tony Blair became leader of the Labour Party in 1994 and prime minister from 1997 to 2007). One of his first acts as party leader had been to ditch the party's ancestral ideological statement with its commitment to public ownership. His New Labour credo was the need to reject the outlook of both the 'old left' (i.e. the Attlee revolution) and the 'new right' (i.e. the Thatcher revolution) in favour of a 'third way' synthesis that reconciled market economics with social justice, individualism with community, and rights with duties. It was impatient with traditional ideological categories, emphasized the need to adapt to a world in rapid and dynamic change ('a world that has taken us by surprise' in the words of Anthony Giddens, a leading thinker of the new dispensation), and insisted that 'what matters is what works'.

It was difficult to pin Blairism down. Its pick'n'mix kind of politics, with lions invited to lie down with lambs, confounded ancestral political arguments. There was much debate about what Blairism 'really' was, a debate which continues to the present day. 'We are not crypto-Thatcherites. We are not old-style socialists. We are what we believe in. We are meritocrats. We believe in empowering all our people. We should celebrate not just those who are born well, but those who do well': this was Blair's own answer. It was an ideology for an age that seemed to have abandoned ideology. It stood for newism. Without coherent alternatives on left or right, it commanded the political landscape and carried all before it. The fact that nobody was quite sure what it was could seem like a positive advantage. Blair's 'big tent' (Figure 4) was deliberately designed to inhabit as much political ground as possible. Internationally, Blair advanced a doctrine of 'liberal interventionism', but this came to grief (as did Blair's own

4. New Labour's 'big tent' (Chris Riddell, *The Observer*, 3 October 1999).

reputation) in the controversy and quagmire surrounding the Iraq invasion of 2003. Yet it was only when the political weather started to get rougher again, as it did with a vengeance once Gordon Brown had taken over from Tony Blair in 2007 and was soon engulfed by the banking crisis, that a new political environment demanded a new set of political responses.

So these were the three ideological tidal waves in post-1945 British politics, at least until very recently. Someone listening in to an imaginary conversation between Attlee, Thatcher, and Blair would soon pick up the dominant political themes of the past century. However, they would also hear something of the wider context of national debate and popular opinion behind these particular arguments. Much of this centred on a continuing and often anguished preoccupation with what was happening to Britain and what it now meant to be British. There was much talk of British 'decline' and how this could be remedied. Attachment to the old struggled with an embrace of the new. Politicians were constantly invoking a 'new' Britain (both Margaret Thatcher and Tony Blair were self-styled modernizers), but this involved a reckoning with the considerable inheritance of 'old' Britain.

The key fronts in this struggle were class, race, and Europe, the salience of which varied at different periods. There was much lively argument for a long period about the extent to which Britain (and especially England) was class-ridden, stuffy, and in the grip of an old establishment, and so needed a thorough shaking-up. The continuing political potency of class was still evident in 2019 as (another) old Etonian was installed as Conservative leader and prime minister. A few years earlier another Conservative, Michael Gove, then education minister, had declared that 'those who were born poor are more likely to stay poor and those who inherit privilege are more likely to pass on privilege in England than in any comparable country'. Then there was the politics of race, which threatened to become incendiary at various points, as British society visibly changed under the impact of large-scale immigration from the old empire (and later from the countries of the European Union under free movement). A Conservative politician provoked controversy by suggesting a 'cricket test' for ethnic minorities (did they support the English cricket team?); while a Labour politician (and foreign secretary) countered by describing Britain as having become a 'chicken tikka masala' society (as this was now its favourite dish). There is nothing more explosive than the politics of identity, and it has lurked just beneath the surface of British politics, testing to the limits a liberal tradition of tolerance and fuelling a politics of racism and anti-immigration that has existed on the fringe of British politics but has had an increasing impact on the mainstream (Figure 5).

It also connects with the issue of Europe, which has been the running sore in British politics for much of the past half-century. It has divided parties and confounded normal ideological positions. Enthusiasts for Europe warned of lost opportunities for Britain ('the history of our engagement with Europe is one of

5. 'Low-minded fears about immigration': a notorious referendum poster whips up fears about immigration.

opportunities missed in the name of illusions and Britain suffering as a result,' declared Tony Blair in 2001); while opponents warned about the loss of sovereignty involved in 'rule by Brussels'. It proved easier to excite public opinion about the threats than the opportunities, aided by a tabloid press that whipped up anti-EU sentiment. The positive case for EU membership went largely unmade, and unheard, and there was no attachment to the European 'idea' that sustained pro-EU sentiment in the rest of the continent.

A founding text for the so-called Eurosceptics was the Bruges speech of Mrs Thatcher in 1988, when she declared: 'We have not successfully rolled back the frontiers of the state in Britain, only to see them reimposed at European level, with a European super-state exercising a new dominance from Brussels.' As European integration advanced, and its difficulties increased, so Euroscepticism turned into Europhobia in sections of the Conservative Party. It became an ideological obsession, threatening to tear the party apart. A party once distinguished by a non-ideological pragmatism now found itself in the grip of an ideology. On becoming Conservative leader, David Cameron had promised to end the party's 'obsession' with Europe, but instead was forced by mounting pressure (both in his own party and the electoral challenge from the UK Independence Party) to announce a referendum on EU membership. In doing so, he declared: 'It is time to settle this European question in British politics.' Instead, like a succession of Conservative leaders before him, it was to end his political career.

He had not wanted to be defined by the issue of Europe. His aim had been to become the 'heir to Blair'. Just as Blair had decontaminated the Labour brand, and made it electorally successful, so Cameron had set about decontaminating the Conservative brand. Where Blair had offered New Labour as his defining idea, Cameron offered a Big Society as his big idea, which he described as being about 'a huge culture change, where people, in their everyday lives, in their homes, in their neighbourhoods, in their workplace, don't always turn to officials, local authorities or central government for answers to the problems they face but instead feel both free and powerful enough to help themselves and their own communities'.

He wanted this to be the *leitmotif* of the Conservative/Liberal Democrat coalition formed in 2010. However, it was soon submerged by the impact of the financial crisis that made its impact felt on British politics for a decade from 2008 onwards. What defined the 2010 coalition government, and the Conservative government that followed in 2015, was not discussion about a big society but its austerity programme and its impact (including whether it was providing a cover for an old ideological ambition to reduce the size of the state). Ideologically, what was on offer was a mixture of fiscal conservatism and social liberalism (the latter most evident in the legalization of gay marriage), but this remained ill defined.

What the financial crash had produced was ideological disorientation on both left and right. The right's belief in free markets and light regulation had been undermined by the irresponsible behaviour of financial institutions and bankers. The left's attachment to a politics of public spending (sustained by tax receipts from Britain's large financial sector) had been undermined by the new politics of deficit reduction. Politicians in all parties lined up to proclaim their attachment to a more responsible version of capitalism. All this was a recognition that something profound had happened, shattering previous assumptions; but it was far from clear where (or when) secure ideological ground of any kind would again be found, what its policy implications might be, and where the centre of political gravity would settle down.

This uncertainty was then compounded by the even more profound disorientation produced by the EU referendum and its aftermath. Despite all the internal party disagreements on the issue at different times, for the previous fifty years every British government, and every prime minister of every major party, had concluded that it was in Britain's interest to be a member of the EU (as it became). Now this consensus was shattered by the referendum. It revealed an attitudinal divide that cut across the traditional dividing lines of British politics. In his vivid account of the referendum (*All Out War*, 2017), the journalist Tim Shipman summed up what it meant: 'If the referendum was anything it was a victory for outsiders over insiders, a dividing line that was replacing both left/right and rich/poor as the dominant split in British politics.' The question may have been about the EU, with those campaigning to leave able to mount a winning 'take back control' alliance that combined high-minded arguments about sovereignty with low-minded fears about immigration; but the answers were about much more. Voters divided by age, education, place, and economic circumstances, but they also divided in their view of the world, with conflicting values and identities. As the referendum was dissected, various attempts were made to describe the nature of the divide. It was a divide that had not been created by the referendum; but it was the referendum that exposed and mobilized it. It might not be the kind of culture war that has come to dominate politics in the United States, but it was nevertheless a clash of cultures that challenged the established ideological contours of British politics. Superimposed on the old ideological axis of left and right was a new axis of liberal and conservative (or open and closed) which seemed to contain even more force.

The parties struggled to respond. They were anxious to get political argument back on to more familiar territory, beyond Brexit, but this proved almost impossible. On becoming prime minister after the referendum, Teresa May had promised a 'one-nation government' and 'a country that works not for a privileged few, but for every one of us'. However this kind of conservatism was lost in the continued austerity, and in the party's civil war on Europe. She tried to revive it in 2018 by announcing that austerity was over, but Brexit dominated everything else (and led to her enforced departure, replaced by Boris Johnson who promised to 'get Brexit done'). At the same time Labour had moved leftward under the unlikely leadership of Jeremy Corbyn, who declared that: 'Today's centre ground is certainly not where it was twenty or thirty years ago. A new consensus is emerging from the great economic crash and the years of austerity. We are now the political mainstream.' Yet the party had its own difficulties and divisions on Brexit, and seemed to many to have abandoned the political mainstream. Others thought the centre ground had been vacated by both main parties, and felt politically homeless. There were defections from both big parties into a centrist grouping, the Liberal Democrats saw an opportunity, while a new Brexit party (the successor to UKIP) made instant electoral progress. The traditional shape of British politics, and the arguments that sustained it, was in disarray. It was against this background that the general election of December 2019 was held. Dominated by Brexit (and the unpopularity of Labour's leader), Boris Johnson's promise of 'getting Brexit done' delivered a big Conservative majority, humiliation for Labour, and a squeeze on the smaller parties (except in Scotland, where the SNP tightened its domination). Boris Johnson promised a 'one nation' government, whatever that time-worn phrase meant, recognizing a need to attend to the working-class communities that his party now represented for the first time. Yet the whole question of what kind of Britain would be created outside the European Union would open up new (or old) political choices. The truth was that nobody was quite sure where the new tide of ideas was to be found, or who would be able to ride it most effectively beyond Brexit. Britain had changed—economically, socially, culturally—and the challenge for all parties was to frame a convincing response.

What was clear though was that the way in which political argument was conducted had also changed. Even before the Brexit referendum, it had coarsened, aided by the new media environment within which politics now operated. The referendum itself made it toxic. Politicians found themselves abused and threatened. Violent extremism was on the rise. When the Labour MP Jo Cox was murdered by a right-wing extremist shouting 'this is for Britain!', the shock and revulsion produced a call for a more tolerant and generous kind of politics. This has yet to arrive. Political argument is not just what is argued about, but how it is argued about. If democratic politics is about the civilized management of disagreement, then British politics after Brexit seemed badly in need of a restorative dose of civility.

Chapter 4
Governing: still the strong centre?

British government is strong government. This may seem a curious statement in view of recent political developments, rendering government weak and ineffective. Yet this has always been the big truth about British politics. It was evident in the response to the financial crisis in 2008. Having authorized a government guarantee of lending to the banks of £186 billion, chancellor of the exchequer Alistair Darling 'reflected that, unlike many of my international counterparts, I had the authority to do so, even if the Bank of England was reluctant, without having first to seek parliamentary authority'. Some people have celebrated this strength, because it gives direction and cohesion to the business of government. Others have lamented it, because it allows government to occupy too much political space and provides inadequate accountability. What we shall have to consider is whether recent constitutional and political changes, along with the environment within which government now operates, mean that this traditional account of strong government needs to be revised. There is also the matter of whether strength is the same as effectiveness. Before that, though, it is necessary to understand the basis for the traditional picture.

In discussing the constitution, we noticed how government had come to occupy the space it did. It was the product of a particular history, in which the centrality of the governing function maintained a continuous existence despite all the other political developments going on around it. This is what Dicey meant when he wrote that 'the prerogatives of the Crown have become the privileges of the people', in the sense that the transition to democracy in Britain had been accomplished while retaining the governing authority historically enjoyed by the Crown: 'This curious process, by which the personal authority of the King has been turned into the sovereignty of the King in Parliament, has had two effects: it has put an end to the arbitrary powers of the monarch; and it has preserved intact and undiminished the supreme authority of the State.' This supreme authority was not pluralized or decisively constitutionalized. Nor was it merely preserved, though, for when government acquired a democratic basis this brought with it a new and powerful legitimacy for its supremacy in the shape of 'the people', represented by ever more organized parties.

It was certainly a 'curious' business. When government in Britain was described as an 'elective dictatorship', this was the indispensable context. In a narrow sense, it reflected the fact that a range of prerogative powers that were formerly possessed by the monarch (for example, to make appointments, sign treaties, declare wars) had transferred intact to the prime minister, bypassing the legislature on the way. There were periodic suggestions that these prerogative powers needed to be constitutionalized in some way, but these were not suggestions that commended themselves to prime ministers or governments, at least until very recently. In a broader sense, the real curiosity of the business is the way in which the executive as a whole retained, and consolidated, its dominance within the political system. It was a top-down polity. This made Britain distinctive among democracies for its degree of concentrated and centralized power.

Leave aside for a moment the question of whether this portrait now requires serious revision, or whether its essential features remain intact. The prior task is to get the original portrait into proper focus. Several elements combined to define the whole. There was the executive's dominance of parliament, and of parliamentary business, in a system with no formal separation of powers. There was an electoral system that eschewed proportionality in favour of the production of 'governments that can govern'. There was the absence of a codified constitution and of a constitutional court to protect it. There was the preference for conventions as the organizing principles of political life. There was the centre's control of the localities, which had no constitutional status of their own. There was a political culture organized around the clash of opposites, in the form of an actual government and a 'shadow' one, rather than a search for consensus, compromise, and coalition-building. There were the tight party disciplines that kept everything (and everybody) in shape.

This is why Britain has been described as the traditional exemplar of a 'power-hoarding' polity. A strong executive centre had not wanted to share power with parliament, other parties, judges, or local governments; and had resisted proposals (for example, to change the electoral system, or to strengthen the second chamber) that would check and circumscribe its governing authority. Behind this predisposition had been erected a legitimizing narrative about the nature of government in Britain. It was the job of the people to elect a government, and it was the job of the government to govern. Nothing should confuse, or get in the way of, the singular clarity of this political arrangement. Crown power had become executive power, and the legislative supremacy established by the House of Commons had secured the unfettered exercise of that power by a majority party. Note the absence in this account of any concern with checks and balances, or with the plurality and division of power, or with competing legitimacies: all the routine stuff of politics and political systems everywhere.

This was not always so. There was a time when good government was thought to require an explicit unbundling of power and accountability. As Peter Hennessy puts it: 'For a few brief years at the beginning of the eighteenth century it looked as if the country might consciously separate the powers of the executive and the legislature.' The 1701 Act of Settlement contained a provision that prohibited a monarchical placeman (a minister to us) from being a Member of Parliament. This provision was repealed (in 1705) before it could be implemented. Had it not been, British government would have developed quite differently. There would have been no easy elision of power from monarch to Cabinet and prime minister, and no fusion of executive and legislature as the operating principle of British government. Even into the 20th century there was a requirement that a Member of Parliament who was made a minister should stand for re-election, a residual attempt to separate out roles, but this too was abandoned once the age of party government had established the ascendancy of the doctrine about a single line of authority and accountability.

So Britain became the home of 'strong government', with a vengeance (see Appendix, Table 3). Formed from a single party (at least since 1945 and until the coalition of 2010), government controlled the House of Commons—more or less securely at different periods—and was able to convert the formal sovereignty of parliament into the effective sovereignty of the executive. That executive is formally a collective one, in the shape of a Cabinet of ministers (supplemented by a larger cadre of subordinate ministers outside the Cabinet). Originally, in fact as well as in name, the King's ministers, they had eventually become ministers without the King as royal power was progressively stripped away. They became instead the ministers of the prime minister, who was formally commissioned to form a government by the monarch ('The Queen has invited me to form a government'), but in practice was the leader of the majority party who appointed ministers (and removed them) as she constructed 'her' government.

Faced with the need, first, to present a united front against the monarch and, later, against parliament and the electorate, a governing convention of 'collective cabinet responsibility' was developed to ensure a common line. As Lord Melbourne told his Cabinet in 1841 as they discussed the Corn Laws, 'we had better all tell the same story'. There have been moments of acute controversy when it has simply not been possible for ministers to tell the same story, requiring the convention to be temporarily suspended (for example, by Harold Wilson at the time of the Common Market referendum in 1975 and by David Cameron during the EU referendum in 2016, and by the Conservative/ Liberal Democrat coalition on the Alternative Vote referendum in 2011). In other circumstances, ministers who want to tell a different story are required to toe the line or resign, as Teresa May vainly tried to inform her Cabinet in the course of the Brexit negotiations.

Well, that's the theory. The practice is inevitably rather different. Even single-party governments contain different views and interests, and opposition parties and the media spend much of their time trying to expose these (while ministers and their acolytes may also brief against each other). Coalition government put additional strain on the convention and required its generous interpretation. Much of the daily political debate in Britain, in the media and between the parties, seems to consist of attempts to show that government (and the 'shadow' government) is not the united front it claims to be. Sometimes it is patently obvious that a government is racked by internal divisions and differences. This was the fate of John Major's government in the 1990s on the issue of Europe (prompting Major to refer, in an unguarded moment, to the group of 'bastards' in his Cabinet).

It was clear that they did not all tell the same story, let alone believe it; but it was also clear that the dissenters could not be removed or disciplined because they merely reflected equivalent divisions within the party. Teresa May struggled with the same issue, though even more acutely, as she tried to negotiate Britain's withdrawal from the EU, with a Cabinet that was openly divided.

In the Blair government, a running theme in all the commentary was the split between Tony Blair's Downing Street and Gordon Brown's Treasury. The language of 'split' (along with the language of 'U-turn') is never far from the British political debate.

Although we talk about 'the government', and the convention of collective responsibility that underpins this, this can be somewhat misleading as a description of how the business of governing Britain actually works. As a former head of the civil service, Sir William Armstrong, once put it: 'The first thing to be noted about the central government of this country is that it is a federation of departments.' Not all departments are equal though, and the Treasury is the most unequal of all. As the keeper of the purse, its tentacles extend everywhere. In the words of a former chancellor of the exchequer, Nigel Lawson, 'it is not for nothing that the Treasury is known in Whitehall as the Central Department'. This also makes the relationship between the prime minister and the chancellor by far the most crucial relationship within government. When it breaks down (as happened between Mrs Thatcher and her chancellor, Nigel Lawson, and between Tony Blair and Gordon Brown), a government is soon in trouble.

Yet it is through individual ministers that the business of government is formally conducted, and it is the ministerial head of each department (the secretary of state) who is charged with the formal responsibility for that department's activity (or inactivity). They have to account to parliament—and to the prime minister, and to the media, and to the wider public—for what their department does. This is what the other governing convention, that of 'individual ministerial responsibility', is all about. It is about carrying the can. Sometimes it may mean resignation when things go badly wrong, but ministers have been more likely to go when they have been found in occupancy of the wrong bed rather than in possession of a failed policy.

They are also likely to have disappeared before their failures come to light. There is perennial discussion about what the 'responsibility' and 'accountability' of ministers actually mean in practice, whether these terms are the same, and how such obligations are properly discharged. Those in search of enlightenment might consult the Ministerial Code, a sort of rule-book on conduct issued by the prime minister to all ministers in the government. This also contains the text of a resolution on ministerial responsibility passed by the House of Commons in 1997, in the wake of an inquiry into the Iraq arms sale scandal. For all its imprecision, the political accountability of ministers is fundamental to the conduct of British politics.

Ministers have all the resources of the civil service at their disposal. This is Britain's permanent government, which has an international reputation for governing integrity. Ministers (and governments) come and go, but civil servants stay. Apart from the small number of politically appointed special advisers that ministers are allowed, and who have become increasingly influential (especially those surrounding the prime minister), the politicians depend upon their civil servants for advancing their policy objectives. A new government does not import a new administration. The deal is that ministers alone are politically responsible for their departments, each of which has a permanent secretary as its administrative head, with civil servants giving loyal service to their minister (of whatever party, bearing whatever policies) in exchange for anonymity and protection of their independence and impartiality. This produces a relationship of serial monogamy between civil servants and ministers (memorably satirized in the television series *Yes, Minister*) that sits at the heart of government. Ministers want results, and quickly; civil servants want practicality, and proper process. This gives rise to inevitable, and necessary, tensions.

There are further tensions between the departmental basis of government and the need for a collective strategy. The Cabinet is the formal mechanism to secure the latter (and can still go 'live' at certain moments, in certain governments, as during the Brexit process), but in practice it increasingly rubber-stamps decisions rather than takes them. It has inherent limitations as a collective decision-making device. Much of the work of Cabinet is now processed through a system of Cabinet Committees, but many of the key decisions that are processed have already been taken in bilateral meetings between the prime minister (or those who act on his behalf) and individual ministers. In the Blair government Cabinet meetings were stripped down to their barest essentials, with the real business of government transacted elsewhere. A joke said to be circulating among ministers at the time asked why only half the Cabinet drank tea; it was because Cabinet meetings were over before the trolley had gone all round the room. Blair started as he meant to go on. On the Sunday afternoon after the 1997 election, the momentous decision to transfer control over interest rates to the Bank of England was taken in a meeting between Gordon Brown and Tony Blair in the front room of Blair's family house in Islington. The journalist Andrew Rawnsley (in his *Servants of the People*) takes up the story of what happened the next day:

> The plan had brought Blair into another collision with the Cabinet Secretary about the centralist style of governing. Handing over control of monetary policy was, by any standards, a sensational step, and the more so because it had not been advertised in advance either to the electorate or anyone else in the Cabinet. When the Prime Minister allowed him into the secret, Sir Robin Butler was astounded to learn that Blair and Brown were planning to act without consulting any other ministers. The Cabinet would not meet until two days after the announcement. Butler suggested to Blair that his senior colleagues should surely be involved in such a momentous change. The Prime Minister was not interested in giving the Cabinet a vote. 'I'm sure they'll agree,' responded Blair. The Cabinet Secretary persisted: shouldn't the Cabinet at least be informed? 'They'll all agree,' repeated Blair, more emphatically.

Butler made a final attempt to convince Blair to follow what Britain's most senior civil servant regarded as the constitutional proprieties. 'How do you know that the Cabinet will agree with the decision when it's still a secret?' Blair replied very simply: 'They will.'

There is endless discussion about whether Cabinet government has now been replaced by prime ministerial government. Each period and each prime minister allows a new twist to be given to this debate. Thus Margaret Thatcher was 'strong', but was eventually brought down by her colleagues. John Major was 'weak', with the Cabinet stronger but with government more ineffective. Tony Blair was 'presidential', which helps to explain why the Cabinet failed to assert itself in relation to the Iraq war in 2003, but this had more to do with a particular conjunction of circumstances—a huge majority, a willing party, a personal authority—than with a permanent alteration in Britain's governing arrangements.

Once the circumstances change, as they can do dramatically, rapidly, and unexpectedly, then so does the centre of gravity within government. Blair's diminished popularity after the Iraq war eventually enabled Gordon Brown and his supporters to force his resignation. Gordon Brown began strong, but his dysfunctional style of governing soon made him very weak; while David Cameron had to negotiate the particular circumstances of coalition government. Teresa May, with no majority and a divided party, struggled to maintain her authority (and was eventually forced to resign). In 2019 Boris Johnson acquired a thumping majority and with it the authority that May lacked (Figure 6). The truth is that a prime minister is both commanding and vulnerable. She dominates the political landscape, but this does not mean that she is in secure and permanent control of all that she surveys. In his memoir of his time in office, Gordon Brown reflected on how every issue 'landed on the doorstep of No.10, no matter what the issue and which department was formally responsible', which was

6. Boris Johnson returns to Downing Street after his election victory, December 2019.

why 'the role of the prime minister has kept expanding and that of the Cabinet has diminished'.

The conventional wisdom in Britain has been that coalition government is necessarily weak and unstable, lacking the cohesion, discipline, and governing authority that single-party government provides. The experience of the Conservative/Liberal Democrat coalition government formed in 2010 challenged this view (certainly if the comparison was with the Brown government that preceded it, or with Teresa May's government that followed it). Rooted in a formal coalition agreement, it combined functioning Cabinet government with an informal system for brokering disagreements. A study by the Constitution Unit concluded that the coalition 'set a model for harmonious and unified government which may prove hard to follow'. Tensions inevitably grew though, with continuing speculation about whether the coalition would hold together for the duration of the parliament. It was a coalition government but not a coalition parliament; and this was the source of its increasing difficulties.

A recurrent question is whether the British system of government by departments, linked by the formal machinery of Cabinet and its committees, lacks an effective centre to hold it all together, ensure policy coherence, and drive it on. Nick Clegg, who was deputy prime minister in the coalition government, has no doubt that 'it is the Balkanisation of authority across Whitehall that is responsible for dysfunctional decision-making'. This is the case for a prime minister's department, which does not exist (part of a prime minister's vulnerability), but which Tony Blair had clearly sought to establish in everything but name both by his governing style and by his development of the Downing Street machine. Blair was much criticized for subverting Cabinet government by an informal and centralizing style of 'sofa' government. However, when David Cameron came to office promising a different governing style it was not long before some of his government's problems were being attributed to a weakness at the Downing Street centre, which he then sought to strengthen.

Nothing so distinguished the Blair premiership as a restless quest for governing levers that worked when they were pulled. Too many of the existing ones turned out to be made of rubber, producing an ever more frantic search for new ones of more durable construction. A civil service that was distinguished by an elegance of governing process met a prime minister whose mantra was 'delivery' of the governing product. It became a charge against the civil service, made by Blair and others, that it was good at keeping the show on the road but much less good at implementing change ('it's great at managing things but not at changing things' was Blair's own verdict).

Policy formulation was not the same as policy delivery, which required a different set of skills. 'The truth is that the British civil service is both a Rolls-Royce and a Morris Minor': this was Nick

Clegg's verdict on his experience of government. Civil servants would have their own story to tell about their frustration with ministers. Making the relationship work well was indispensable for good government. It worked best when there was clear political direction, so that civil servants knew what was expected of them, and when ministers stayed in post long enough to get on top of the job. But there is a paradox here. A system of 'strong' government, the traditional hallmark of British politics, too often combined with a weakness of practical delivery capability. Governing capacity, in a political sense, was not the same as policy effectiveness. That is why the Johnson government elected in 2019 declared its intention to shake up the civil service and change the way in which government operated.

This directs attention away from the narrow terrain of the political centre to the wider world of 'governance' in Britain. This is the world of executive agencies, quangos, partnerships, regulators, contractors, and all the rest of the dense and complex network of arrangements through which government now operates. The central executive, even when it can negotiate its own fissiparous tendencies, depends upon this vast and unwieldy apparatus for converting its policy ambitions into administrative results. This development has been described as the 'hollowing out' of the state; and it is certainly very different from the traditional model of public administration. It is more like a hub-and-spoke system, involving the management of increasingly complex chains of delegation and accountability.

It is scarcely surprising that a pull on the central levers can often seem to produce only a muffled and uncertain response. The Blair government (and Gordon Brown's Treasury in particular) initially seemed to believe that they could micro-manage everything from the centre, setting targets, controlling funds, and imposing disciplines. This is what 'strong government' permits. However, they soon discovered that this was far more difficult in practice than they had allowed for; and the emphasis began to switch to developing 'strategic capacity' at more local levels, with 'earned autonomy' for organizations which could demonstrate good management and delivery.

The 2010 coalition government led by David Cameron promised a radically different approach to governing, involving a rejection of statism and centralism. 'We want to turn government on its head,' declared Cameron, 'taking power away from Whitehall and putting it in the hands of people and communities.' The coalition agreement promised 'radical devolution of power and greater financial autonomy to local government and community groups'. Instead of 'bureaucratic accountability' there would be 'democratic accountability'. Previously the emphasis had been on deploying all the resources of a strong centre to force improvement in how the state delivered its services; now the emphasis was on getting the state out of the picture and enabling others to take on the job.

So Whitehall numbers were culled, business outsiders brought in to oversee departments, and policy advice contracted out. In the name of localism, local government was given more flexible powers and community groups more powers in relation to local government. In the name of accountability, all items of public spending would have to be logged and published. There would be elected police commissioners and public services like schools and hospitals increasingly freed from state control. A bonfire of quangos saw a range of public bodies either abolished or merged. Here was the centre wanting to offload responsibilities, but in the event it did not represent a lasting transformation in how Britain was governed. Its critics alleged that it was really just about reducing the size and role of the state.

Part of the intention was to disperse power so that the central state would no longer be looked to for solutions to every problem. Yet this ran up against a political culture in which equity was preferred to diversity and the state was expected to provide a uniform level of service to its citizens wherever they lived (without a 'postcode lottery'). This made the rhetoric of localism easier than its practice; while projections indicated that demands on the state, especially from an ageing population, were set to increase sharply in the future. There was also the enduring force of the political tradition of ministerial responsibility, which demanded accountability from government even if provision had gone elsewhere. In this sense a strong centre was rooted not just in control of the levers of government but in an established culture of expectations. Changing the latter was more difficult than releasing the grip of the former.

If the centre has been especially strong in Britain, it is at least in part because other centres of power have been especially weak. Local democracy has been consistently eroded as the centre has tightened the screw. Although local government had never enjoyed any formal constitutional status, unlike the position of subnational governments in much of Europe, it had traditionally been protected by a custom and practice of separate spheres (once described as a 'dual polity') in Britain's informal constitutional arrangements. This changed sharply in the last two decades of the 20th century, when the centre snuffed out the vestigial independence of local government (the crucial constitutional moment was the 'capping' of local spending and taxing by the Thatcher government in the 1980s) and trampled all over the old conventions.

The great bulk of local authority spending now comes from the centre, which inevitably erodes the basis for a vibrant local democracy. The 'localism' of the Cameron government did not extend to restoring the taxing and spending power of local government. Similarly, although Scotland, Wales, and Northern Ireland now have forms of devolved government, England has not developed a devolution structure of its own, although the arrival of elected mayors in city regions with their own funding packages may prove to be a first step in this direction. For the moment, though, all roads still lead to the centre.

If the British system is one of strong government, it also has some evident weaknesses. The strength comes from a political system in which the executive has been in routine control of parliament, and where institutional checks and balances of a formal kind have been largely absent. In this sense government in Britain has been exceptionally, even uniquely, strong. It has commanded a wide political territory, with a large freedom of action, and possessed a formidable ability to translate policy ambitions into legislative achievements. This made a British prime minister (at least one with a secure majority) much less hemmed in, and constrained, than many other political leaders elsewhere. Strong government of this kind gives a capacity for action, both at home and abroad, that represents a substantial asset. This being so, it may seem perverse to talk of associated weaknesses.

Yet these exist. Capacity for action is not the same as policy effectiveness. Post-1945 British history is distinguished by a running lamentation about the failure to halt decline, deal with entrenched problems, or keep up with other countries. This led some to suggest that the British system of alternating 'strong' governments produced policy lurches, policies that were poorly scrutinized, and a failure to build durable consensus in key areas. Countries with much 'weaker' governments seemed, perversely, to have done rather better. A best-selling book by Anthony King and Ivor Crewe was able to document a long list of *The Blunders of our Governments* (2013), suggesting 'that there are systemic defects in the British system of government, defects rooted in the culture and institutions of Whitehall and Westminster'. The National Audit Office regularly reported on projects failing and money wasted.

So too with the centralization of the British system, which enabled government to ensure that its writ ran everywhere without check or hindrance, but also meant that there was a paucity of other institutions with the capacity for effective action. An ever more frantic pressing of buttons at the centre was a reflection of the weaknesses associated with such a lop-sided governing strength. An ever more complex network of control chains and coordinating mechanisms was required in an effort to keep the governing show on the road, and these often proved ineffective.

Then there were the changes from other directions, which posed huge challenges to the traditional British way of governing and required new governing techniques to be learnt. Engagement with the institutions of the European Union, which had formed an ever-increasing part of the lives of both ministers and civil servants, introduced a pluralistic world of bargaining, negotiation, compromise, and coalition-building which was in stark contrast to the winner-takes-all model of executive dominance which distinguished the domestic political terrain. A tradition which boasted a 'sovereignty' that insisted on a single and inviolable source of governing authority met a tradition in which power was for sharing if this advanced the capacity for collective action. As Britain negotiated its exit from the European Union, these traditions collided.

Other changes came from nearer home, many of them a consequence of the constitutional reforms introduced by the Blair government after 1997. Their combined effect was to impose new checks on government and more pluralism in governing. Handing control of interest rates to the Bank of England imposed a major economic check. The Human Rights Act 1998 introduced a fundamental judicial check, involving a new discipline for the whole of government and bringing the courts into the business of government far beyond the judicial review of administrative action that had already grown in size and scope in the preceding years. The Freedom of Information Act 2000 brought a stronger informational check, involving a formal break with a traditional culture of secrecy and a wider window on the activities of government.

Further checks came from new rules on party funding, and from new regulatory bodies like the Electoral Commission and official watchdogs such as the Committee on Standards in Public Life and (since 2010) the Office for Budget Responsibility. New conventions, such as the use of referendums for major constitutional changes, also became established. At the same time parliament was becoming more assertive, chipping away at prerogative powers on matters such as war-making, treaty-making, and public appointments. All this meant that ministers and governments were far more constrained than they had once been.

Then there was the pluralizing of government, the conversion of a unitary state into a union state, that came with the creation of new forms of government in Scotland, Wales, and Northern Ireland (and with electoral systems that pluralized power in the same way that the Westminster system concentrated it). There was no longer a single British political system, but several political systems within Britain, while externally whole tracts of policy had become controlled or circumscribed by the European Union. Governing involved negotiating this new reality.

The referendum decision to leave the European Union promised a recovery of control, but its immediate effect was to present British government with its biggest modern challenge. There had been no preparation for it. The withdrawal process had been triggered without any developed plan for what came next. The civil service duly swung into action, consuming all the energies of Whitehall in the process, but in the absence of clear political direction it was difficult for it to know what it was preparing for. When it tried to fill the void, it was attacked for its efforts.

The negotiating process was bogged down by political disagreement about what leaving the EU actually meant. There was no attempt to respond to a narrow referendum outcome (a margin of only 3.8 per cent) by building a cross-party consensus on how to proceed, in a situation in which the government had no parliamentary majority and parties were divided. The effect of all this was an appearance of governing chaos, in relation to an issue that had momentous implications for the whole future of the country. One minister, on resigning, described 'a failure of British statecraft on a scale unseen since the Suez crisis'. In fact it was much more serious than that crisis sixty years previously. 'Has the country ever been so badly governed?' asked Polly Toynbee in her *Guardian* column (13 November 2018), a question asked by many others. Where was the strong centre when it was most needed? Britain's reputation for good government seemed to have been shredded.

So the old portrait of a system of strong government clearly needs some revision. Britain's political system is still, in comparative terms, a power-hoarding one, with supports for a strong centre remaining in place. Yet the supports are much weaker and the governing constraints much stronger. When governments fail to command parliamentary majorities, then the problem intensifies. When Boris Johnson became prime minister, he was soon confronted by the fact that he had no majority and that parliament had to be reckoned with. It was only when he won a secure majority that his position changed, and with it the recovery of a governing strength and stability that had been lost. The question is whether it is still possible to describe Britain as the home of strong government. If not, this would be a remarkable development.

There is a wider issue too. As former prime minister John Major put it in his memoirs: 'Governments can cajole, entice or plead, but they can no longer control.' At least until recently Britain has remained a well-governed country, certainly in comparative terms, but with notable weaknesses. Yet the real challenge to strong government, as the financial crisis provided a brutal reminder, was from sources of power that individual national governments seemed unable or unwilling to control. Along with issues like climate change, this seemed to require action beyond the nation state, at a time when nationalism was resurgent. This was the challenge for governments everywhere and Britain was no exception. That was why its decision to leave the European Union raised the question of whether, although it promised more control, in practice it might produce the opposite.

Chapter 5

Representing: voters and parties

It used to be very simple to describe the British version of representative democracy. In elections voters chose the candidate of the party they wanted to represent them in parliament and the party with a majority of seats then formed a government. Each of the main governing parties represented different sections of society. The job of elected representatives was to support their parties in parliament, which was where politics was conducted and sovereignty resided. Parties presented programmes to the electorate and these policies were then represented in government. Between elections voters had no further formal involvement in the business of government, which was a matter for their representatives, until another election involved them again.

We shall have to discuss how much of this picture remains true, and how much has changed. Clearly the EU referendum has raised fundamental questions about the relationship between representative democracy and direct democracy ('our experiment in direct democracy is hurtling towards our tradition of representative democracy like some giant asteroid towards the moon,' wrote *The Times* columnist Matthew Parris after the referendum); but even leaving that aside there were significant ways in which the representative system was changing. Much of this change centred on parties and the party system, along with changes in the behaviour of voters.

Parties are fundamental to representation. If you want to get elected in Britain, at least in general elections, then you have needed to get a party (and a party with some chance of winning). The occasional and isolated exceptions only prove the rule. Before the 2010 general election, in the wake of the parliamentary expenses scandal, there was speculation that independent candidates might do unusually well, but in the event this did not happen. The fallout from Brexit produced defections from both Conservative and Labour parties, but the defectors faced the challenge of contesting an election without a party (or joining another party, or stepping down) and none of them won in the 2019 general election. Elected politicians have a wonderful capacity for persuading themselves that their electoral success is to be explained by their obvious personal qualities, but the evidence is all against them. Overwhelmingly, it is the party label that counts. British politics is party politics. This is one of the big truths. Yet parties themselves have been becoming weaker and the traditional party system less secure, which raises the question whether this traditional picture requires some revision. This is something to which it will be necessary to return.

Following the 1997 election, legislation was introduced (Registration of Political Parties Act 1998) to enable parties to register the title to their name, and to similar names that might confuse the voters. The significance of this legislation was not what it contained, which was relatively minor, but the fact that legislation on political parties had been introduced at all. This was a major constitutional departure. The role of political parties might be one of the big truths of British politics, but it was a truth that had hitherto not dared to speak its name. Apart from some small housekeeping provisions, the existence of political parties was a closely guarded constitutional secret. This was like describing a car without mentioning that it had an engine.

It was not until 1969 that party names were even allowed to appear on ballot papers, finally exploding the fiction that it was individuals rather than parties who were being voted for. In the House of Commons the fiction is still maintained by the absence of any party designation in the way that MPs are formally described. They are simply the 'Honourable Member' for a particular constituency. The real business is done through a mysterious device known as the 'usual channels' where the party managers carve things up between themselves away from the decorous party-blind formalities of the chamber. But party has now come in from the constitutional cold. The legislation on party registration was followed by a flurry of other measures—including party list electoral arrangements for devolved assemblies and regulation of party funding—that brought the parties and the party system into full view.

So the secret was out. In Britain party rules. The centrality of party to the operation of the political system is fundamental. Tony Blair became prime minister in 1997 because in 1983, just three weeks before the general election, a few members of the Trimdon branch of the (then) safe Labour constituency of Sedgefield persuaded the 83-strong general committee of the local party, by the wafer-thin margin of 42 to 41, to add the young barrister's name to the shortlist from which it was selecting a parliamentary candidate. This is a vivid illustration of the way in which the parties act as the gatekeepers and recruiting agents of British political life. Governments are formed from among the tiny pool of politicians who belong to the majority party in the House of Commons. These politicians are there not primarily because of the electorate but because of a prior election held by a small party 'selectorate', whose choice is then legitimized by the wider electorate.

In other words, the parties control the political process. While this is a feature of political life almost everywhere, in Britain the control exercised by the parties is exceptionally tight. Ever since

Jonathan Swift satirized a Lilliputian world divided between High-Heelers and Low-Heelers (the issue at stake being the size of heels on shoes) and Big-Enders and Little-Enders (where the dispute is over which end of an egg should be broken first), the party question has been endlessly debated. Some saw party in terms of the evils of faction and sectionalism; others as (in Edmund Burke's words) 'a body of men united, for promoting by their joint endeavours the national interest, upon some particular principles in which they are all agreed'. The movement from loose associations of interests and persons to tightly organized electoral and parliamentary machines is the story of the development of the modern party system. It was a development that transformed political life. In the 1840s Sir James Graham, Peel's Home Secretary, described 'the state of Parties and of relative numbers' as 'the cardinal point', for 'with a majority in the House of Commons, everything is possible; without it, nothing can be done'.

The crucial period of transition was the 19th century. Some have looked back nostalgically to a mid-Victorian 'golden age' before the grip of party had tightened, when governments could be made and unmade by shifting coalitions of parliamentary support; but what it meant in practice was rather different. In his *The English Constitution* (1867) Bagehot described the 'impotence' of political life without organized parties: 'It is not that you will not be able to do any good, but you will not be able to do anything at all. If everybody does what he thinks right, there will be 657 amendments to every motion, and none of them will be carried or the motion either.' This is a text that could hang above the desks of chief whips everywhere, and could be a commentary on the Brexit process. It was after the 1867 Reform Act that party organization really took off, in response to the challenge of an enlarged urban electorate. Mass democracy produced mass parties (a process described by Ostrogorski in his *Democracy and the Organisation of Political Parties* (1902) as the 'methodical organisation of the electoral masses'). This aroused hope in some, and fear in others.

Parties are the organizers of political choice. This is a crucial function in any political system. In Britain the modern range of choice was shaped in the decade following the end of the First World War in 1918, with the final arrival of (near) universal suffrage, the disappearance of troublesome Irish representation after the creation of the new Irish state, and the emergence of the infant Labour Party in place of the Liberals as the main alternative to the Conservatives. We became so accustomed to the post-1945 world of strong single-party governments and a two-party political system that it was easy to forget that an earlier world was quite different. Coalitions and minority governments were normal and the disciplines of party weaker (strikingly evidenced in the political career of Winston Churchill, who first left the Conservatives for the Liberals, then later moved back again). As the Jenkins Commission (set up by Tony Blair to look at the electoral system, as part of his deal with Liberal Democrat leader Paddy Ashdown) put it in its 1998 report: 'On the factual record it clearly cannot be sustained that…there is anything shockingly unfamiliar to the British tradition about government depending upon a broader basis than single-party whipped votes in the House of Commons.'

So the 'British model' was of more recent vintage than often supposed. On a long view perhaps it was the post-1945 world that was the aberration rather than the norm. At the beginning of the 1920s Britain had a three-party system; by the end of the 1920s it had effectively become a two-party system. At the general election of 1923 the Conservatives won 248 seats, Labour 191, and the Liberals 157; at the 1929 general election the equivalent figures were 249, 287, and 59 (and it was downhill all the way for the Liberals for decades after that). It was after 1945 that the British model of a 'classical' two-party system, the bedrock of 'strong' government, came into its own. The duopoly of two parties was established. From 1945 until 2010 Britain was governed either by the Labour or Conservative parties. At times majorities were fragile or even non-existent, but single-party government was sustained. When the Conservatives won the 2019 election with a large majority, it was after a decade of government without a secure single-party majority and nearly three decades since the party had been able to form a majority government after an election.

It was in the generation after 1945 that Britain came closest to the pure model of two-party politics. During this period over 90 per cent of all votes went to the two main parties (peaking at 97 per cent in 1951). Class, ideology, and party seemed to have established a tight fit. Labour got its votes from the working class; the Conservatives from the middle and upper classes. In fact it was never quite as tight as it seemed (there was the 'anomaly' of the third of working-class people who voted Conservative, and evidence of disconnection on some issues between voters and 'their' parties), but it was probably as close as it could reasonably get. A textbook writer in the 1960s could confidently assert that 'class is the basis of British party politics; all else is embellishment and detail' (Pulzer). Then, after 1970, it all began to fall apart. On the surface it might seem the same, with governments still formed from one or other of the two big parties, but underneath there was radical discontinuity. Party competition went on as before, but the relationship between the parties and the electorate had undergone a profound change.

This is most strikingly seen in the sharply diminished share of the vote taken by the two main parties. Still at 89 per cent in 1970, this figure dropped to 75 per cent in 1974 and never recovered in following elections (and dipping to 65 per cent in 2010). It was only in the 2017 election that this trend went into reverse. In the 2015 election the two-party share of the vote was just over 67 per cent; but in 2017 it jumped to over 82 per cent. In the 2019 election it was 76 per cent. It remains to be seen if this represents a genuine return to the ascendancy of two-party politics (with Scotland always the exception), or a reflection of the exceptional condition in which British politics found itself at the time.

Labour's electoral nadir had come in 1983, with only 28 per cent of the vote (and only 32 per cent in 2019); while the Conservative nadir came in 1997 with 31 per cent. Another way of telling this story is to record the fact that from the 1970s elections were being won on a share of the vote that would have lost elections in the generation after 1945. The Conservative 'landslide' victory of 1983 was built on a vote share less than its share in the 1964 election when it lost; and Labour's landslide wins of 1997 and 2001 saw its share of the vote lower than when it lost badly in 1959 (see Appendix, Table 2).

The reasons are not hard to find. Other parties were more in evidence and took more votes. Between 1945 and 1966 in half the seats only Labour and the Conservatives put up candidates, but from 1974 all seats were contested by at least three parties. The Liberals received a boost with the SDP split from Labour in the early 1980s, while the nationalist parties in Scotland and Wales strengthened their position. The advance of the nationalists in Scotland was most striking, with the SNP replacing Labour as the dominant party in Scotland, culminating in its landslide victory at the 2015 election when it won 56 out of 59 seats (slipping back in 2017, but then advancing again to take 48 of the 59 Scottish seats at the 2019 election). Parties of the right (UKIP) and of the left (the Greens) added to the mix. Of these minority parties, the anti-EU UKIP attracted most support, winning nearly 27 per cent of the vote at the 2014 European parliament election, but finding it difficult to win even a single Westminster seat. However, its level of support threatened the other parties (particularly the Conservatives) and helped to bring about the EU referendum, for which its reward was a virtual wipeout at the 2017 election (its support down to under 2 per cent, from over 12 per cent in 2015).

The more other parties prospered, so support for the two major parties fragmented. This was illustrated most dramatically at the elections to the European parliament in 2019, which saw the lowest two-party share of the vote in any election to the parliament, while the just-formed Brexit party topped the poll and the Liberal Democrats came second. This produced much speculation about a possible reordering of British politics. However, within months the picture was sharply different, as these minor parties were snuffed out at the general election as two-party dominance reasserted itself.

Yet the underlying fragmentation remained. There was a loosening of the link between class and party ('class dealignment' in the jargon) with 63 per cent of people voting for their 'natural' class party in the 1964 election but only 41 per cent by the 2005 election). In the 2017 election class had virtually disappeared as an indicator of party support (replaced by age as a more reliable indicator). The same pattern was even more evident in the 2019 election, where age and education were decisive factors and the Conservatives won over the lowest-paid and least educated voters. This represented a huge change in the social basis of British politics, evident too in the 2016 EU referendum.

There had also been a marked weakening over this same period in the attachment felt by voters towards parties (in the jargon 'partisan dealignment'), which saw over 40 per cent of voters identifying very strongly with a political party in the 1960s but only 14 per cent doing so by 2015, with the number expressing no attachment doubling over this same period. This is reflected in the unprecedented level of voter switching between the extended array of parties in the most recent elections, as revealed by the work of the long-running British Election Study. In 2015 43 per cent of voters had switched from the party they supported in 2010; and in 2017 33 per cent had switched from their vote in 2015. Gone were the stable allegiances that had sustained the party system in the past, replaced by a volatility that contributed to the instability of British politics and the unpredictability of election outcomes. The dramatic outcome of the 2019 election, transforming the political landscape as traditional allegiances were abandoned and Leave-voting working-class areas turned to the Conservatives, was a reflection of this changed electorate. The 'floating voter' was no longer a small component of the electorate but a wide swathe. Twice as many people are now attached to the opposing Brexit tribes as they are to political parties. Put these trends together (and add in declining party membership) and the cumulative picture of weakening parties becomes clear.

Yet for a long time this was concealed from view by a first-past-the-post electoral system that preserved the two-party dominance of the House of Commons. Only in Scotland was this dominance broken. British politics therefore looked the same, even though it was not. In 1983 the combined vote share for Labour and the Conservatives fell to 70 per cent, but this still delivered them 93 per cent of the seats (and the Liberal Democrats, only a whisker behind Labour in votes, won a mere 23 seats to Labour's 209). The electoral system saved the two-party system. As long as the main parties retained this dominance, even when they were on the ropes, it was difficult for a third party whose support was evenly distributed to break through. This has always been the problem for the Liberal Democrats; and it is why UKIP could not convert its electoral support into seats at Westminster. By contrast, in Scotland the SNP benefited from its defined territorial focus.

The mismatch between a declining two-party system among the electorate and its survival at Westminster could be viewed in different ways. On one view what was being propped up was a party system that failed to represent the changed disposition of the electorate. However, on another view, it could be seen as serving to protect the stability of the political system against fragmenting tendencies that would render effective government more difficult. The 2017 election result might have seen a dramatic return to two-party dominance, confirmed by the 2019 election in which Brexit played a key role, but the underlying trends remained the same.

7. **Winner takes all** (*The Guardian*, 26 May 1990).

There was a symmetry between a traditional winner-takes-all system of government, in which a governing majority in the House of Commons enjoyed largely unchecked power, and a winner-takes-all electoral system that, at least until recently, usually delivered victory to a single party (despite the fact that no winning party since 1935 had secured over 50 per cent of the votes) (Figure 7). Put together, here is what 'strong government' in Britain has traditionally meant. It has given unshared power to a party, and then given all the governing resources of a weakly constitutionalized polity to that party. This was winner-takes-all twice over. When a party government had a crushing majority in the House of Commons (as the Conservatives had in the 1980s, and again after 2019, and Labour after 1997, prompting speculation in these cases about whether two-party politics had become one-party politics), then it was even three times over.

The 2010 election, which failed to give a governing majority to any party, was the moment when the post-1945 party system finally succumbed to the erosion of its electoral foundations. In this sense the arrival of coalition government was not so much an aberration as a culmination. Not only did it bring Britain in line with the European norm, but it brought Westminster in line with what was happening in the rest of the United Kingdom. It is no longer possible to describe something called 'the party system' in Britain, as there is now a variety of party systems. In Scotland and Wales (and with even more intricate power-sharing arrangements in Northern Ireland) there are new kinds of electoral systems producing new kinds of governing systems. They are multi-party systems; and coalition politics has become routine (as it has in tracts of local government). All that had traditionally been seen as alien by the party system at Westminster, and as the unfortunate political habits of foreigners, had become the normal way of doing politics, now including Westminster too.

Coalition government subverted the established conventions of political life, which were wonderfully simple and straightforward. They found their legitimizing ideology in the doctrine of the mandate and the manifesto. A party told the electorate in its election manifesto (once a short and broad statement, now a long and detailed prospectus) what it would do if elected; and then claimed to have a mandate from the electorate for its actions in government.

The claim is spurious of course, at least in any precise sense, but that does not make it less potent. Manifestos are package deals, making it impossible to know which individual items are supported or disliked. The mandate rolls everything up together without discrimination. This enables politicians to claim that they 'have a mandate' for a particular policy when they may well have nothing of the kind, on the basis that the policy in question was 'in the manifesto'. How could anyone possibly oppose something that the people had given a mandate for? Yet the mandate was really only an authority to govern.

Coalition complicated the way in which parties had been able to exploit the resources of the British tradition of strong government. The arrival of democratic politics, and along with it the modern party system, had bestowed a new legitimacy on this tradition by providing a direct transmission belt from the people's will to party government. Parliamentary sovereignty could now be identified with popular sovereignty, and the practical expression of both was the sovereignty of party (although there was a coyness about describing it in these terms). If party was the carrier of the people's will, then it was clearly right that it should hold unmediated sway. After all, who could gainsay the mandate bestowed by a sovereign people? The problem for a coalition government was that it did not have this kind of mandate, as it was a post-election arrangement made by the politicians. It therefore had to advance an argument of necessity to justify its existence. If coalition government became normal, it would not be possible to describe the representative process in the same old way.

Party has inserted itself into every nook and cranny of British political life. The parties control the process of political recruitment, nationally and locally, and by extension also control (although now with some checks) the vast world of appointed government that sits alongside the narrower world of elected government. It is the patronage of party leaders that puts people into the House of Lords. Parties structure the policy choices that are put to voters. They produce the political leaders who form governments and oppositions. They organize the election campaigns. The whole of political argument in Britain is dominated by a permanent election campaign between the parties. Because each of the main parties aspires to form a government, in an electoral system that gives priority to government-forming over opinion-representing, they have to make a broad electoral appeal. This has meant that the coalitions that were absent from the formal face of British politics from 1945 to 2010 were ever-present in the internal life of these catch-all parties, which span a wide range of interest and opinion. They have to try to give an appearance of unity, even though they might be far from united (as Brexit illustrated dramatically) and racked by internal dissent.

The right of local parties to choose parliamentary candidates (in all parties) is jealously defended. The national party machines would much prefer to draft their own favoured people in if they could get away with it, and try various means to do so, but the local party selectorate remains firmly in charge of this gateway to political careers (and, on occasion, the exit route). There have been isolated experiments with primary elections involving the wider electorate, and provisions for a recall procedure in certain limited circumstances, but nothing that significantly alters the picture of party control. This is why the prospect of deselection by local parties has become a major factor in the internal controversies in both Labour and Conservative parties, exacerbated by Brexit, and why party realignment is so elusive. Politicians know that losing (or leaving) their party is almost certainly a career-ending move.

All this raises issues about how the local party selectorate operates and what kind of representatives it produces. The rise of the Labour Party in the early years of the 20th century was in part a response to the refusal of local Liberal associations to select working-class candidates. Later in the century the making of 'new' Labour included a move to 'one member one vote' in candidate selection to break the hold of constituency activists who were regarded as unrepresentative of the party's members and voters. The embarrassing paucity of women being selected by all the parties prompted Labour to introduce women-only selections in some constituencies for the 1997 general election, producing a doubling in the number of women MPs. The whole question of how representative politicians are of the people they represent has received growing public attention in recent years, requiring the parties to respond.

What has happened is that politics has become an overwhelmingly middle-class occupation, with almost everyone having had a university education. But the major parties represent different kinds of middle class: the Conservatives come typically from a business background, Labour from the public sector. The working class has virtually disappeared from parliamentary representation: at the 1966 election 30 per cent of Labour MPs had been manual workers, but by the 2017 election this had plummeted to only 5 per cent. There had been changes on the Conservative side too: in 1951 78 per cent of Conservative MPs had been privately educated, but this had dropped to 48 per cent in 2017, below half for the first time (though still wildly unrepresentative of the wider population).

After the 2019 election diversity increased further, with more women and ethnic minority representation and with MPs less likely to have been privately educated or gone to Oxbridge than after any previous election. Where there has been growth is in the number of MPs who had previously worked in politics, rising from 3 per cent in 1979 to 17 per cent in 2015 (and this is probably an underestimate). This seemed to indicate the development of a class of professional politicians, without wider experience, something which prompted comment and concern. The most striking change though was in the representation of women. In 1979 only 3 per cent of MPs were women; but in 2017 this had risen to 32 per cent, the highest figure ever. In some respects at least, British politics was beginning to look more like the society it represented.

How the parties organized themselves raised other representational issues. These issues have historically been most acute in the Labour Party, for the party was the product of an extra-parliamentary movement that was organized on the basis of internal democracy. This brought endemic and inevitable tensions between the parliamentary leadership and the wider party. Some even questioned whether Labour could function as a 'normal' parliamentary party. By contrast, the Conservatives were a resolutely 'top-down' party in which leaders were supposed to lead and followers to follow. The sharply different character of the annual conferences of the two parties used to serve as a vivid reminder of their respective internal cultures and structures.

Then all this changed, as the parties began to operate in very similar ways. Although members might be asked to approve major policy documents, and be entitled to vote for party leaders, control and direction became firmly centralized in both the Labour and Conservative parties (rather less so in the case of the Liberal Democrats). More recently, these trends seem to have gone into reverse. Conservatives have exchanged loyalty for dissent, unafraid to cause trouble for their leaders. Labour has reverted in spectacular fashion to a breach between its parliamentary party and its newly enlarged and radicalized membership. Its members elected a leader that the parliamentary party did not want and thought was unelectable, and in whom the parliamentarians passed a no-confidence motion, but who could not be removed because he was kept in place by the votes of the members in the party's internal democracy. When leaders are chosen by party members, if those memberships are so diminished or unrepresentative that they do not reflect wider opinion then the consequences for political leadership are serious. Boris Johnson became prime minister in 2019 because of the votes of a Conservative membership that was small in number and doubtfully representative.

This directs attention to the memberships of the political parties (and how representative they are). There has been a long-term decline in party membership, with Britain having one of the lowest party membership rates in Europe. By 2010 only 1 per cent of the electorate was a member of one of the main parties, compared with nearly 4 per cent in 1983. In the 1950s the Conservative Party had some 3 million members; in 2019 it had just 160,000 members (most of whom were elderly), fewer even than the Scottish National Party. Labour had experienced its own decline, from over a million members in the 1950s to only 190,000 in 2013.

Yet while membership decline had been the story for the main parties, other parties (UKIP, the Greens, and especially the SNP) had been increasing their membership, especially in the years after 2013. So had the Liberal Democrats, despite their electoral collapse in 2015. But the most striking recent membership revival has come with the Labour Party, starting with its leadership election in 2015 and aided by a reduced rate membership system. By 2018 the party had over half a million members, who were able to install and maintain a leader of their choice. Membership of the Conservative, Labour, and Liberal Democrat parties, which had dropped to a historic low of 0.8 per cent of the electorate in 2013, increased to about 1.6 per cent in 2018. In Scotland SNP membership increased from 0.6 per cent of the electorate to around 3 per cent over this same period. It was difficult to know if this rise in membership of the political parties marked a permanent reversal of the trend of decline, or if it reflected the political turbulence (Brexit, the Scottish independence referendum) of a particular period.

Parties are indispensable to the political process, yet 'party politics' has long been a routine term of political disapprobation in Britain. As Sidney Lowe put it: 'No sentiment is likely to elicit more applause at a public meeting, than the sentiment that "this, Mr Chairman, is not a party question, and I do not propose to treat it from a party standpoint"' (*The Governance of England*, 1904). Edmund Burke's famous speech in 1774 to the electors of Bristol, in which he announced that he was their representative but not their delegate, was difficult to transpose into an age when representatives had largely become the delegates of party.

If politics without party is a recipe for impotence and chaos, the domination of politics by party brings its own problems. As society changes, it becomes harder to claim that parties are the uniquely legitimate channel of political representation. It is sometimes observed that the Royal Society for the Protection of Birds has more members than all the political parties put together. At one level this simply reflects the fact that people prefer birds to politicians, which is clearly not an irrational preference, but it also points to a dichotomy between a society which is ever more diverse in its composition, attachments, beliefs, and interests and a political process in which the parties retain a tight grip.

Of course in practice there is a vast representational network through which society presses its extraordinary (and often conflicting) range of demands and interests upon the politicians, and the parties are required to broker all this into some kind of politically manageable form. That is an absolutely vital function. It is also why some of the attacks on party are badly misplaced. Yet in the British context it does make sense to ask if party claims too much political and representational territory. The fact that the vast majority of people in Britain do not belong to a political party, and have diminished attachment to party, raises questions about the role of party as the gatekeeper of all public life. The disciplines of catch-all parties can also make them very blunt representational instruments. If the major parties move in directions which make them less representative (which is a charge levelled at both Conservative and Labour parties), then more people will feel politically homeless. At the same time both Conservative and Labour parties have found it increasingly difficult to keep their internal coalitions together. This prompts regular speculation that the party system might be reconfigured and realigned, although how this might come about remains unclear.

The biggest challenge to the party-based representative system has come from the EU referendum. The system was designed to demarcate the space between governing and being governed. It was the job of the electorate to put governments in and to boot them out; but it was the job of the politicians to do the governing. Thus the conventional political wisdom in Britain had been that the referendum was a dangerous foreign device that was incompatible with the British system of parliamentary representation. It was associated with demagogic populism and the techniques of tyranny. As Clement Attlee declared in 1945: 'I could not consent to the introduction into our national life of a device so alien to all our traditions as the referendum.' Mrs Thatcher echoed this view. Yet now the modern conventional wisdom is that major constitutional changes should routinely be approved by referendum (Table 1).

This constitutional innovation originated as an expedient to contain internal Labour divisions over the European issue in the 1970s, just as in 2016 it was resorted to by the Conservatives in a bid to contain their own deep divisions on Europe. In this latter case, though, it brought consequences that convulsed the political system. It split parties, fractured loyalties, and raised questions about the whole party system.

Some welcomed this exercise in direct democracy, in which the turnout had been much greater than at the previous or subsequent

Table 1. UK-wide referendums

Year	Question	Result	Turnout
1975	Do you think that the United Kingdom should stay in the European Community (the Common Market)?	Yes 67.2% No 32.8%	64%
2011	At present, the UK uses the 'first past the post' system to elect MPs to the House of Commons. Should the 'alternative vote' system be used instead?	Yes 32.1% No 67.9%	42.2%
2016	Should the United Kingdom remain a member of the European Union or leave the European Union?	Remain 48.1% Leave 51.9%	72.2%

Note: In addition to these UK-wide referendums, there have been referendums in Scotland, Wales, and Northern Ireland, London, and the North-East region of England, and in local authority areas. In 2014 Scotland held a referendum on whether Scotland should be an independent country, with 55% to 45% in favour of remaining within the UK, on a turnout of 85%.

general elections. If it subverted the system of representation by party and parliament, then so much the better. Thus Vernon Bogdanor, an enthusiast for government by referendum, announced that 'the sovereignty of the people is trumping the sovereignty of parliament' and that 'the referendum has now established itself as a third chamber of parliament, issuing legislative instructions to the other two'.

Others thought that this was dangerous nonsense, and that it had been irresponsible to allow the future of the country to be decided by a narrow majority in a politically inspired referendum based on specious claims which, even if it brought damaging consequences, could not (unlike elections or votes in parliament) be easily reversed. It had also produced a populist kind of politics in which politicians claimed to speak for 'the will of the people' even though people were clearly divided on the issue. On this view the referendum confirmed the virtues of representative parliamentary democracy, which was called upon to deal with all the consequences of the referendum decision (including what it really meant). Whatever else it had done, the referendum had brought the whole question of representation into sharp focus, with consequences that are still working themselves out.

Chapter 6
Accounting: parliament and politicians

Democracy has accountability at its heart. In a democracy government is expected to be accountable to the people. This happens through elections of course, but also through a continuous process of holding to account. It is not just the ability to kick a government out that defines a democracy, but also the ability to kick a government while it is in. It has to be held to continuous account for its actions and inactions. That is why, in assessing any political system, a question to be asked is how effective it is at the business of accountability. So what can we say about British politics in this respect? In particular, how does a political tradition that has been marked by an attachment to strong government combine this with the requirements of accountability?

In his *The English Constitution*, Bagehot coined a striking phrase to describe the importance of a clear line of accountability when he declared that 'the sovereign power must be *come-at-able*'. In other words, the responsibility of government should be readily identifiable, thus enabling it to be held to account for what it did. For a long time this ability to combine effective government with clear accountability was seen as a distinguishing attribute of the 'Westminster model'. It was based on an essentially simple conception of an accountability chain, with ministers accountable to parliament and parliament accountable to the people. It was the clarity of this line of accountability that was seen as its strength, which was why there was resistance to proposals that seemed to muddy the line.

One such proposal was the reform of the electoral system. The first-past-the-post system might have deficiencies in terms of representation, but it was claimed that this was more than made up for by what it delivered in terms of accountability. The electorate voted for a party that formed a government, which was then either re-elected or rejected at the next election. In this way elections performed their central accountability function, in a system in which there was a clear line of accountability between governors and governed (even if there was little accountability of individual politicians, especially those in 'safe' seats, insulated by party labels from personal accountability). Unlike in other systems, accountability could not be dodged or fudged. It had a brutal simplicity to it. Of course the main parties defended the electoral system for reasons of political self-interest, but the accountability argument was usually called in aid. It was only when the electoral system ceased reliably to produce majority governments that this argument became less convincing to deploy.

As we shall see, there are all kinds of ways in which governments are held to account, but there is one institution which is charged with the constitutional function of continuous political accountability. This is parliament; and the question to be asked is how effective it is at performing this function. It certainly gives the appearance of doing its job. This job is not to initiate, which is the role of government, but to scrutinize and pressurize. As Gladstone said of parliament in 1855, 'its business was not to govern, but to call to account those who govern'. If accountability is about asking questions, getting information, and demanding answers, then parliament does this in spades. In many ways it functions as a great accountability machine. Questions are asked and answered, statements made and examined, debates conducted, inquiries undertaken, legislation scrutinized, and votes

93

taken. Misleading or misinforming parliament is the gravest ministerial sin, for which the highest political penalty is demanded. Governments can only survive if they command sufficient parliamentary support, as tested by a vote of confidence. All this constitutes a formidable armoury of parliamentary accountability, reflecting the primacy of the constitutional doctrine of the sovereignty of parliament.

Perhaps the most visible expression of accountability in action is the daily interrogation of ministers, and weekly of the prime minister. This can be a daunting experience. Tony Blair was very good at it, but he has nevertheless described it in his memoir as 'the most nerve-racking, discombobulating, nail-biting, bowel-moving, terror-inspiring, courage-draining experience of my prime ministerial life, without question'. However, he then added that 'it's also rather a myth that it's a great way of holding the prime minister to account'. In other words, the appearance of accountability may not reflect the reality. If parliament engages only in a ritualized kind of accountability, then this makes it less effective than it might be.

Once the ceremonial veneer is stripped away, and the rhetorical fog of parliamentary sovereignty is allowed to clear, the fragility of accountability in a system in which the government has routinely controlled the legislature produces a more complicated picture. A weak parliament has been the other face of strong government. This is why, in the latter part of the 20th century, it became commonplace to argue that the executive was too powerful and insufficiently checked, especially by parliament. What this meant in practice was once nicely described (by the former MP Austin Mitchell in his splendidly entertaining *Westminster Man*) as like 'heckling a steamroller'. The heckling was loud and raucous, but the executive steamroller took it all in its stride and got on with its governing business. It might not always be smooth, but the bumpy bits were a small price to pay for undisputed occupancy of the wheel. That, at least, was the traditional picture. We shall need to ask if the recent history of parliament (and politics) has modified this picture in any significant way; but only after saying something about the context within which parliamentary scrutiny operates.

In some ways it is misleading to refer to 'parliament' at all, as though it had a collective identity. It is useful for governments to be able to describe it in this collective way ('parliament has approved this measure', etc.), because it confers legitimacy on executive actions, but it is inaccurate as a description of how parliament is organized and operates. Parliament in a collective sense does not really exist, or only sporadically. What does exist is a place where government and opposition meet to do battle in the permanent election campaign that defines and dominates British politics. This is why, when parliament as a whole was called upon to act in the Brexit saga, it found it very difficult to do so. It required collaboration across party that went against the grain of normal parliamentary politics.

This means that its scrutiny function is conditioned by the context within which it operates. With no formal separation of powers, the executive routinely controls the legislature (even if at times with difficulty). Governing without a majority, as both the May and Johnson governments discovered, means a loss of this ability to control. In normal times Members of Parliament are not primarily scrutineers, but government-supporting or opposition-supporting party politicians. This is why the daily question time to ministers, and once a week to the prime minister, has taken the form it has. It is the daily opportunity for the rival parliamentary armies to lob custard pies at each other (although the most lethal ones come from stroppy members on their own side). Much of the continuous scrutiny and accountability that takes place is undertaken by the opposition, which is a valuable function, though with a necessarily partisan character. It is easier being a vigorous scrutineer of government from the opposition benches than from the government's own side, although governing party MPs have more opportunity to raise concerns and apply pressure from the inside. The informal face of parliamentary accountability is the continuous need for a governing party to keep its parliamentary supporters on board. This is why 'dissidence' in the division lobbies, which has steadily grown, only captures the formal face—and failure—of a continuous process of intra-party political accountability. When MPs are asked to rate the importance of scrutiny among their various roles, it is unsurprising that it gets a higher rating when their party is in opposition and a lower rating when their party is in government.

The daily life of the House of Commons reflects the dilemma of accountability in a political system with fused rather than separated powers between executive and legislature. The fact that the results of parliamentary votes are routinely known in advance (with the Brexit process as a striking exception) gives a sterile quality to much debate. In fact 'debate' is really a misnomer for what are usually prepared speeches served up to a largely empty chamber in which neither minds nor votes are likely to be changed by what is said. This gives a ritual character to proceedings. It would be nice to record that the 1935 diary entry of 'Chips' Channon, then a new Conservative MP, is a historical eccentricity: 'Most of the day at the House of Commons. Today for the first time I really liked it; boredom passed and a glow of pleasure filtered through me. But I wish I sometimes *understood* what I was voting for, and what against.' Alas, it is not. It is only on those occasions when an issue divides parties, and makes the result of votes uncertain, that the chamber springs into life. In recent years there have been an increasing number of such occasions, culminating in the parliamentary dramas of Brexit.

The extent to which parliament (and crucially the House of Commons) is less effective than it might be as an instrument of accountability is most apparent in its scrutiny of legislation. In outward form legislation is carefully scrutinized through an elaborate series of parliamentary stages, including detailed consideration in committee. The reality is that the whole process is firmly controlled by the government, serious scrutiny by government members is actively discouraged, any concession or amendment is viewed as a sign of weakness, and the opposition plays a game of delay. There is no shared commitment to making legislation as good as it can be. The result is that much legislation is defective, vast quantities of amendments have to be introduced by the government in the House of Lords (where, even in its semi-reformed state, scrutiny is taken more seriously), and the government's control of the parliamentary timetable means that many of these amendments are then simply voted through by the Commons without any scrutiny at all. It is all deeply unsatisfactory, and felt to be so by almost everyone involved in it, although recent detailed research on the legislative process (by Meg Russell at UCL's Constitution Unit) paints a rather more positive picture of the variety of ways in which parliament can influence the process.

This takes us back to the wider context. On one view, here is a political system in which scrutiny is embedded and in which accountability is relentless and often ferocious. On another view, though, here is a system in which neither scrutiny nor accountability is as effective as it might be. At bottom, this is because most (though not all) members of the legislature have an ambition to join the executive. Parliamentary foot soldiers dream of one day carrying a ministerial baton. There is therefore an intrinsic problem of accountability, beyond the routinized accountability of adversarial party politics. This is why the textbook talk about parliament's role in scrutiny and accountability frequently fails to get inside the skin of an institution many of whose members have a different set of priorities.

Contrary to common belief, the power of the party whips is the consequence, not cause, of such considerations. Members generally vote for the party line not because they are coerced to do so but because they want to. It is also the route to advancement, in a system which (at least in the past, before the modern development of the select committees) has had no parliamentary career path except joining the executive (or shadow executive). This contrasts sharply with countries where the legislature is stronger and more independent. Just in terms of numbers, the executive's hold on parliament in normal times is tight (and has become tighter over the years), as between a third and a half of the members of the governing party in the House of Commons are effectively on the executive's 'payroll' vote and subject to the disciplines of collective responsibility. Executive control on this scale necessarily saps the independence of the legislature. It is not just that most Members of Parliament have a desire to join the executive, but that this desire can be accommodated to a significant degree.

Of course Members of Parliament have many fish to fry. Lacking a job description, or any measure of performance, they have to work out for themselves how to do the job. The result is that the job is done in many different ways. There are loyalists and mavericks. There are those who see parliament as their priority, and those (a growing band in recent times) whose main focus is on their constituency. There are those who are never heard of; and those who are never unheard of. There are the duds and the diligent. There is plenty to keep MPs busy, but whether it is busyness with a purpose, or the busyness of a hamster on a wheel, is another matter. This question was asked by Gyles Brandreth, who had a spell as a Conservative MP in the early 1990s, one of those 'scurrying like dervishes round the bottom of the greasy pole', who recorded this in his diary at the end of one parliamentary day: 'We're here every day, from breakfast till midnight . . . darting from one committee to the next, signing letters, tabling questions, meeting constituents, being busy, busy, busy—but, frankly, to how much avail? . . . I've not stopped . . . But really, was there any point to it all?' At a basic level, therefore, the extent to which parliament is effective in its function of scrutiny and accountability depends upon whether Members of Parliament take this part of their role sufficiently seriously.

It is sometimes suggested that parliament does much better on the accountability front when it comes to the system of select (or scrutiny) committees which monitor the general work of government, mainly mirroring departments, and which have developed in their modern form since 1979. There is some truth in this. These committees conduct inquiries and issue reports, and attempt (unlike the rest of the Commons) to operate on a consensual and bipartisan basis. It was believed that these committees would be able to keep a much closer eye on what ministers and officials were doing than was possible in the political theatre of the Commons chamber, and this has proved to be the case. However, they have suffered in the past from a number of important limitations. Political commitment to them was weak, they offered no parliamentary career structure, resources were limited, and (most significant of all) their members were appointed by the party machines. It was only after the parliamentary expenses scandal of 2009 that changes were made to strengthen the select committee system. A Reform Committee declared that it was time for the Commons to become 'more vigorous in its task of scrutiny and accountability' and proposed that the select committees (and their chairs) should be elected and that backbenchers should control more of the Commons business.

The fact that these committees and their chairs had been appointed by the party machines—the scrutinized appointing the scrutinizers—was stark evidence of parliament's accountability deficit. Making the change to election not only gave them more independence but raised their profile and gave them a new energy. They now put themselves at the centre of the big issues of the day in televised hearings, demanding the attendance of witnesses who would often have preferred not to be held to public account. Armed with their new legitimacy, and with the election of some independent-minded chairs who would not have emerged under the previous whip-appointed system, the select committees have become major players in British politics. Those who chaired them have become public figures in their own right, with the committees offering a career structure in parliament that does not depend upon joining the executive.

However, the committees also have weaknesses. They vary in their quality. Some can be uncoordinated and unfocused in the way they operate. They are not well equipped to undertake the more forensic investigation of issues that other kinds of inquiry are called upon for. Sometimes the desire to be at the centre of every political issue can be at the expense of more prosaic scrutiny work, with a lack of sustained focus. In many ways the committees are still works in progress. Perhaps most fundamental of all, MPs still need to commit themselves to their scrutiny function as a central activity. However, there is no doubt that the evolution of the select committee system does represent a significant improvement in parliament's account-holding capability.

In fact, from a number of directions, the accountability role of the Commons has been strengthened during the first two decades of this century. Changes to the public bill committees that examine legislation, enabling evidence-taking, have brought at least the possibility of better scrutiny and improved legislation. There is more draft legislation and pre-legislative scrutiny. The select committees have acquired a role in vetting major public appointments. Parliament has reined in prerogative power on war-making and treaty-making (and on the calling of elections). Prime ministers now have to appear regularly in front of a parliamentary committee. At the same time the Commons has more control of its own business, producing debates and votes on issues (like an EU referendum) that both government and opposition would have preferred to keep off the parliamentary agenda. All this represents some shift in the terms of trade between parliament and the executive, in which strong government begins to be matched by stronger accountability.

It may even be time to stop lamenting the decline of parliament from some mythical golden age, usually located somewhere in the middle of the 19th century (a period more accurately described by Gladstone at the time as 'the paralysis of Parliament'), and start registering its recent rise.

For much of the 20th century it was commonplace to lament the 'decline' of parliament, with MPs described as having become mere lobby-fodder for their parties. 'As things are now', wrote Christopher Hollis in his 1949 book *Can Parliament Survive?*, 'it would really be simpler and more economical to keep a flock of tame sheep and from time to time drive them through the division lobbies.' In the 1960s a seminal study of British politics by the American political scientist Samuel Beer (*Modern British Politics*) observed that party cohesion at Westminster had become 'so close to 100 per cent that there was no longer any point in measuring it'. Yet this ceased to be true almost as soon as it was written.

From the 1970s onwards dissidence began to grow and in recent years has accelerated. This reflected a weakening of the ferocious tribalism that had been sustained by sharp ideological division. As party allegiance weakened in the electorate, it became less plausible to sustain it in parliament. The Blair government's decision to take military action against Iraq led, in March 2003, to the biggest party rebellion in the division lobbies in modern parliamentary history. The habit of dissidence grew among Conservative MPs during the post-2010 coalition government, fuelled by antipathy to their coalition partners. In 2013 the government was defeated by backbench rebellion when it asked the Commons to approve military action against Syria.

But it was the issue of Europe, culminating in Brexit, that took dissidence to a new level of intensity. It produced the biggest defeat for a government in modern parliamentary history, with a 'party within a party' of hard-line Brexiters who refused to toe the line. Loyalties had become much more fluid. As government proved incapable of governing, lacking a majority, parliament tried to take control of the Brexit process (aided by an activist Speaker) and in some respects succeeded. This was a remarkable constitutional development. The control of parliamentary business by government, the hallmark of the governing system, was challenged by a new parliamentary assertiveness.

None of this means that parliament, like other institutions, has not declined in importance over time as others have taken over some of its functions. Ken Clarke, who has been in the Commons for half a century, reflected in his memoir *True Blue* (2016) how he had spent his career 'observing the steady decline of Parliament's influence on public life'. But at the same time it no longer fits the supine stereotype that used to be applied to it. As the dramas of Brexit showed, provoking a new parliamentary assertiveness, there is plenty of life in the old dog yet. It remains to be seen if parliament will continue to assert itself after the return of majority government and the conclusion of the Brexit saga, and whether the spirit of independence and cross-party cooperation will endure, or whether this period will come to be seen as the transient response to an exceptional set of circumstances and followed by parliamentary business as usual.

Then there is the House of Lords. There is always the House of Lords (Figure 8). Ever since the Parliament Act 1911, which reduced the power of the Lords to that of delay, declared a future intention 'to substitute for the House of Lords as it at present exists a Second Chamber constituted on a popular instead of hereditary basis', the matter of House of Lords reform has been one of the hardy annuals of British politics. Over the last two decades there has been a royal commission, committee reports, white papers, joint committees, draft legislation, bills, debates, and votes. The result of all this activity has been the removal of most (but not all) of the hereditary peers and with them the entrenched Conservative majority in the Lords. What has not resulted is any agreement on how this semi-reformed and bloated

8. 'There is always the House of Lords...' (Peter Brookes, *The Times*, 12 July 2012).

Lords, now appointed largely by the patronage power of party leaders, might move through a promised 'second stage' of reform to its final shape. A House of Lords reform measure was part of the Conservative coalition deal with the Liberal Democrats in 2010, promising a predominately elected second chamber, but when a bill was produced in 2012 giving effect to this it had to be abandoned in the face of concerted Conservative opposition. It was yet another episode in the long saga of failed Lords reform.

Yet even in its semi-reformed state, the Lords has become more assertive (and successful) in getting the Commons to think again about aspects of legislation. In this sense the Lords has also added to the strengthening of accountability that has taken place in the Commons, so enhancing the accountability capacity of parliament as a whole. Much of the debate on Lords reform has centred on the respective merits of election and appointment, and the implications for legitimacy, but this is not the only consideration. There is broad agreement that a deliberative second chamber, able to revise and review, adds to the armoury of accountability in Britain. It should be neither rival nor replica of the Commons, but a partner. Instead of seeing a more legitimate and confident Lords as a threat to the primacy of the Commons (which, in terms of powers, it could not be), it would be more sensible to see it as strengthening the scrutiny and accountability role of parliament as a whole. It could also play an important role in a federal constitution. However, none of this makes comprehensive reform of the Lords any easier politically, which is why reform has come (if at all) only incrementally. It would require a huge investment of political capital and energy on the part of a government to drive radical reform through in the face of entrenched resistance.

It many ways this focus on parliament in relation to the business of holding power to account is rather misleading. It reflects traditional constitutional doctrine rather than current political reality. Accountability operates in a whole variety of ways and through many different channels. Simply to focus on parliament as the formal arena of accountability is clearly inadequate. For example, the media play a key role in exposing and investigating. A grilling on the *Today* programme or a mauling on *Newsnight* is often a much more formidable (and visible) exercise in accountability for a politician than what happens in the House of Commons. Instead of the media feeding off parliament, as was once the case, it is now common for parliament to feed off the media. Then there is the whole army of regulators, auditors, inspectors, inquiries, and watchdogs which now preside over every nook and cranny of the public realm (and those parts of the private sector which are deemed to have a public interest). The accountability role of parliament has been supplemented by a dense thicket of largely extra-parliamentary devices to monitor the activities of government. Many of these were established in the two decades from the mid-1990s; and it is no exaggeration to describe this period as witnessing an accountability explosion, as this summary outline makes clear:

Ethical watchdog: Committee on Standards in Public Life established as standing ethical watchdog on standards of conduct in public life, with accountability as one of its Seven Principles of Public Life.

Elections and party funding: Rules on party funding, donations, and election spending introduced, monitored, and enforced by an Electoral Commission.

Human rights: Human Rights Act incorporates European Convention on Human Rights and enables human rights issues to be heard and decided by the courts.

Information: Freedom of Information Act gives right of access to official information, supported by an Information Commissioner. Open data provisions and performance information on public services. Legislation to protect whistleblowers.

Public appointments: Public appointments by ministers governed by a code of practice and monitored by a Commissioner for Public Appointments. Vetting of major public appointments by select committees.

House of Commons: Resolution on ministerial accountability adopted; new powers (previously prerogative) on war-making and treaty approval; election of select committee chairs and members and control of backbench business.

Parliamentary standards: Parliamentary Commissioner for Standards established to monitor financial interests and code of conduct, and to investigate complaints about MPs. Independent Parliamentary Standards Authority established to regulate MPs' expenses and remuneration, and to enforce compliance with the rules. Recall provision for MPs introduced for serious misbehaviour.

House of Lords: Appointments Commission established to appoint independent cross-bench peers and to vet all peerage nominations for propriety, including nominations from the political parties. Scrutiny role strengthened by removal of most hereditaries.

Judges: Establishment of independent Judicial Appointments Commission strengthens judicial independence by removing role of Lord Chancellor; and establishment of Supreme Court transfers judicial authority from House of Lords.

Civil service: Civil Service Commission put on statutory basis (previously prerogative) to protect civil service values under the Civil Service Code.

Prime minister: Publication and revisions of Ministerial Code, with a prime minister's independent adviser on ministers' interests to investigate alleged breaches; and convention established that prime minister appears before a committee of select committee chairs on regular basis.

Statistics: Establishment of UK Statistics Authority to safeguard integrity of official statistics by independent scrutiny and monitoring, including investigation of alleged abuses.

Referendums: Convention established that major constitutional changes require referendums, with their operation—and the questions—regulated by the Electoral Commission.

Security Services: Parliamentary oversight of security services introduced by establishment of Intelligence and Security Committee.

Economy: Interest rate policy transferred to independent Monetary Policy Committee of Bank of England; and Office of Budget Responsibility established as independent fiscal watchdog.

Fixed-term parliaments: Legislation on fixed-term parliaments introduced, replacing prerogative discretion on dissolution exercised by the prime minister.

Complaint, inspection, and regulation: Proliferation of ombudsman-type complaint and redress schemes (including independent complaints body for the police) and new inspectorates and regulators.

It is only necessary to produce a quick list of this sort to see how accountability mechanisms of assorted kinds have expanded over the last two decades. It also serves as a reminder of how unconstrained government in Britain has been in the past. A traditional accountability, through parliament, seems to have been replaced by a plethora of regulators and inquirers and inspectorates. Parliament has been an onlooker, not a participant, in this process. If parliament is to perform its function of holding power to account, it should not pretend (as it once did) that it can substitute for other forms of accountability; but it should take steps to ensure that it sits at the apex of this accountability structure. Holding power to account should be a continuous process, on a variety of fronts and involving a range of bodies, but this whole process should be pulled together by the formal institutions of representative democracy. For what parliament, uniquely, can insist on is *public* accountability.

Where does all this leave ministerial accountability? This is the traditional way in which political accountability in Britain has been described, with officials accounting to ministers and ministers accounting to parliament. It remains an axial principle, but the context in which it operates has undergone significant change. The size, complexity, and fragmentation of modern government make it more difficult to identify a direct line of accountability. In 2016 the National Audit Office issued a report on accountability in which it warned that it was becoming more difficult for Accounting Officers (the civil service heads of departments) to account properly to parliament. As chair of the Public Accounts Committee, Margaret Hodge MP was frustrated by the difficulty of pinning down responsibility, finding the doctrine of ministerial accountability an impediment and concluding (in her book *Called to Account*) that 'it is the doctrine of ministerial accountability that is broken and needs fixing'. Nor are these abstract issues, for they go live every time there is political dispute (especially when things have gone wrong) about who is responsible for what.

It might have been supposed that the expansion of accountability mechanisms in the last two decades would have produced more confidence and trust in government. This was often announced as its purpose. Yet the reverse has happened. As accountability has increased, so trust has declined. No doubt there are many reasons for this (including the scandal of MPs' expenses and the financial crash), but it nevertheless remains something of a paradox. Perhaps it is best explained by the fact that the multiplication of accountability has produced a sense that direct, visible, and effective accountability has become more elusive. 'Never before in British history', observed Anthony King in his *The British Constitution*, 'have so many individuals and organisations been so comprehensively accountable to so many other individuals and organisations . . . Where everyone is accountable to everyone else, it is always possible that no one is effectively accountable to anyone.' There is more accountability, but for less. In other words, despite all the developments in accountability, power is less directly 'come-at-able' than it once was.

Partly this is because government has sought to hive off its own responsibilities, with a deliberate de-politicization of decision-making. Whatever the merits of this, it has produced a sense that power has escaped from democratic control. Government has to explain its diminished role as power has passed to new places and new bodies. However, the sense of loss of control goes much wider and deeper than this, as much that determines the lives of citizens now seems beyond the control of democratic politics. If politics is unable to hold all kinds of power to account, then consequences will follow. In the 2016 Brexit referendum a major theme was that the EU was unaccountable to the electorate and that power—and therefore accountability—should be returned to the national state. This was a powerful argument, expressing a basic democratic instinct of the British. As Teresa May expressed it (in her Florence speech in September 2017): 'The strength of feeling that the British people have about this need for control and the direct accountability of their politicians is one reason why throughout its membership the United Kingdom has never totally felt at home being in the European Union.' However, others thought that the effect of leaving the European Union would make the accountability of real power much harder to achieve.

Chapter 7
Whither British politics?

Before the general election campaign of 2017, the Political Studies
Association surveyed over 300 political scientists and other
'experts' on their prediction of the election outcome. They all
forecast a big Conservative victory, with most expecting a majority
of over 100 seats. When the election produced no overall majority
and a hung parliament, it was a major shock. Yet this was only
the latest in a series of shocks. The 2010 general election had
failed to produce a majority government, resulting in the un-British
experience of coalition. The general election of 2015 was not
expected to produce a majority government, but it did. In Scotland
it produced a landslide for the SNP, wiping out Labour's historic
dominance at a stroke. The referendum on the EU in 2016, with the
leaders of all the mainstream parties and most expert opinion on the
side of staying in the European Union, was not expected to produce
a vote to leave, but it did. In the general election of December 2019
there was therefore caution in making any predictions, but the
result was nevertheless astonishing. The only certain thing about
British politics was that it had become uncertain. It was foolhardy
to venture confident predictions about what would happen next,
or what the future shape of British politics would look like.

Recent years had seen political turbulence on all sides. Both
Labour and Conservative parliamentary parties had tried to

depose their recently elected leaders, and the Conservatives had succeeded. In January 2019 the government suffered the biggest defeat in modern parliamentary history on its Brexit plan. Party loyalties fractured. Collective Cabinet responsibility disintegrated. There was wide agreement that the country was experiencing a political and constitutional crisis. What was remarkable was the short space of time in which all this had happened. The 2010 general election may have failed to produce a majority, but the coalition government that was formed (the first since the Second World War) functioned quite well as a government and lasted a full term. In 2011 the *New York Times* columnist David Brooks, writing from London, could tell his readers that Britain provided 'a picture of how politics should work' and that 'the British political system is basically functional while the American is not'. Yet only a few years later the general verdict was that Britain was 'a case study in political dysfunction' (Rafael Behr, *The Guardian*, 30 October 2018).

So what had happened? The short answer is Brexit (there is a longer answer). The referendum in June 2016 unleashed shock waves that rocked the political system to its foundations. Representative democracy collided with direct democracy, parliamentary sovereignty with popular sovereignty, with consequences that nobody had thought through or planned for. The binary choice in a referendum offered no guidance about the further choices involved in its implementation. The withdrawal process was triggered and a departure date set before there was any developed plan about how to proceed. Politicians struggled with competing legitimacies. Parliament found it difficult to find a coherent voice that would influence the process. In the absence of clear political direction, the civil service floundered. The government seemed unable to advance an agreed negotiating position, much to the frustration of the EU. Its energies were largely consumed by negotiating with itself and its parliamentary supporters.

When the history of this period comes to be written (and no doubt an inquiry held), it will be necessary to explain how the most important policy decision in post-war British history came to be decided in the way that it was. The referendum was intended to solve a problem for the Conservative Party, not to create a problem for the country. For thirty years the issue of Europe had divided the party, with the anti-EU forces steadily gathering pace. It had contributed to the downfall of three Conservative prime ministers, with Teresa May as the fourth. There were regular predictions that, like the Corn Laws fissure in the middle of the 19th century, the party would eventually split on the issue. Faced with this mounting pressure, and with UKIP snapping at Conservative heels, prime minister David Cameron decided that the promise of a referendum was the only way to defuse the issue. When he achieved an unexpected majority at the 2015 election, he then had to redeem his promise. In one sense, he was successful. He had shot the UKIP fox and kept his party together, at least for the moment. Some argue that he had no alternative as party leader but to follow the course he did. Yet the consequences for the country were momentous, and he failed in his task of keeping the country in the European Union. Nor did the referendum end the Conservative Party's civil war on the issue, but for several years made it even more intense.

In fact the way in which the Brexit process was handled, with its focus on party management, reflected the British way of doing politics. A narrow referendum result, with the country divided down the middle, might have been seen to require some coalition-building in order to put together a consensus on a version of Brexit that could command wide support, find the parliamentary centre of gravity, and repair the deep divisions that the referendum had created. As the referendum decision had merely established the principle of leaving the EU, but said nothing about the terms on which this might be done, this left ample opportunity for such an approach. Countries in the EU with whom exit negotiations were conducted, many of which had responded to their own deep divisions by developing a political culture of compromise and accommodation, found it difficult to understand why the British did not now follow a similar path. The EU itself functioned on the basis of consensus-seeking among its members. Yet this was not the British way. Instead of cross-party collaboration in response to exceptional circumstances, both government and opposition settled for a traditional adversarialism (with only a belated and doomed attempt at bridge-building). Prime minister Teresa May, faced with a choice between seeking common ground and splitting her party, opted to appease her party. Her party reciprocated by removing her.

What all this would mean for the future of British politics prompted much speculation. What the Brexit parliamentary process had revealed was that there were Members of Parliament who had more in common with each other than with their respective parties. They developed a habit of cooperation, largely unknown previously. Some left their parties in order to work together. There were Conservatives of the 'one nation' tradition who repudiated the party's hard-line Brexiters, while there was a large chunk of the parliamentary Labour Party that repudiated their party leadership. Normal party disciplines collapsed. This inevitably invited speculation about party realignment, with a new party being formed on the common ground. This also seemed to reflect a feeling of political homelessness on the part of many in the electorate. Whatever else it had done, Brexit had given the discussion of realignment a new lease of life.

Yet it did not make it any easier, or more likely. There was a reason why the party system had remained so durable, despite the erosion of some of its foundations. In Britain, with its simple plurality electoral system, it was very hard for a new party to break through. Although there had been splits before, not since the replacement of the Liberals by Labour in the particular circumstances following the First World War—and with the introduction of near-universal suffrage—had the party system been fundamentally reconfigured. The Social Democratic Party breakaway from Labour in the 1980s had electoral successes for a while, but old party loyalties soon snuffed it out. In a presidential system (as in France) it proved easier for a new entrant to break through, and in a multi-party proportional electoral system more parties can get their feet in the door. British politicians know all this, which is why risking their jobs (and their salaries) in the cause of a new party—however desirable they might regard it—is seen by most as a risk too far. Whether the enormity of Brexit would change this calculation was much debated. In some ways the electoral conditions were more propitious than they were a generation earlier, when party loyalties were stronger and class voting more entrenched. Brexit had fractured parties, but in the event the party system had nevertheless survived.

There was wide agreement that the Brexit saga had exposed failings in the political system. As *The Times* put it: 'Chief among the problems that Brexit has unearthed is a political process that is no longer working as it should' (4 February 2019). Some argued that British politics was broken. The Hansard Society's annual audit of political engagement in 2019 found more public dissatisfaction with the system of government than at any time in the survey's history, along with majority support for a strong leader who was prepared to break the rules. Political leadership was lacking, in both government and opposition, and the party system blocked sensible cooperation. The business of government was consumed by Brexit, at the expense of a range of other pressing issues. In many ways Brexit provided an object lesson in how not to conduct politics or run government. If this was so, might the fallout from Brexit include a restructuring of the political system? Would a political tradition that relied on muddling through be so shaken by what had happened that it was prepared to embrace systemic reform? Might it even be the moment when some serious constitution-making was embarked upon? At least for a time, these were the questions on the table (Figure 9).

9. The end of British politics? (Ben Jennings, *The Guardian*, 29 March 2019).

Before such questions can be answered, it is necessary to be clearer about the nature of the problem. Britain had certainly experienced a political crisis, but was it also a constitutional crisis? In many respects the famous flexibility of Britain's uncodified constitution should have enabled politicians to respond to whatever was thrown at them. This was the traditional claim. The fact that they had such difficulty in doing so was primarily a political failure, not a constitutional one. It was a failure of the political class and of the party system. A political tradition that had prided itself on its statecraft, which was thought to make a codified constitution unnecessary, seemed to have lost the political skills that had been its hallmark. Where constitutional reform had recently been enacted, in the form of the 2011 Fixed-term Parliaments Act, this was seen as inhibiting political flexibility. Yet at the same time Brexit had identified a range of constitutional issues that demanded attention.

Perhaps the most obvious was the need to think seriously about referendums and about how they fitted in with a system of representative democracy. When might they be used? Should they be only advisory? Should there be rules about turnout and the size of the majority? What could be done to ensure reliable information? Was better regulation of funding and campaigning required? These were not abstract questions, as the EU referendum had raised them in the most acute form. It exposed the lack of preparation. It pitted majority opinion in the country against majority opinion in parliament. It brought doctrines of popular and parliamentary sovereignty into irreconcilable conflict. It also produced the hitherto unknown spectacle of a government deliberately implementing a policy that its own analysis showed would be damaging to the country's economy because it had been instructed to do so by 'the people'. Some argued for another referendum to test the decision of the first; while others wanted no more referendums at all. The issue of their place, if any, in a representative democracy could not be avoided.

However, Brexit had also raised other constitutional issues. The relationship between parliament and the executive had been brought into sharp focus, as parliament struggled to insert itself in a system where legislative business was in the exclusive control of government. The intervention by the courts in curbing prerogative power, and insisting on the rights of parliament, pointed in the direction of a new constitutional role for the judiciary. A constitution that relied upon conventions to make it work ran into trouble if these conventions were not observed, raising the question of whether they needed the reinforcement of codification. The inability of the party system to find common ground, or to represent significant bodies of opinion in the country, suggested a need to explore whether a remedy might be found in a reformed electoral system. On top of all this, and in addition to previously unfinished constitutional business (like the House of Lords), there was the vast enterprise of scrutinizing the mountains of post-Brexit legislation and regulations in a constitutionally satisfactory way. If action was not taken to prevent it, the effect of Brexit could leave rights unprotected and executive power strengthened.

Then there were all the tensions generated by the referendum outcome in the different countries of the United Kingdom, where both Scotland and Northern Ireland had voted to stay in the European Union. Not for the first time the Irish question inserted itself into British politics, as border issues threatened to undermine the peace process, with consequences for the future of the constitutional settlement itself. It was possible that one eventual effect of the referendum would be to advance the cause of a united Ireland. In the case of Scotland, already with a strong independence movement, it seemed possible that a British exit from the European Union would increase the chances of a Scottish exit from Britain. After the 2019 general election the stage was set for a constitutional clash between the SNP government in Scotland, which claimed it had a mandate for an independence referendum, and a Conservative government at Westminster that resisted this claim. The prospect therefore was of the United Kingdom disintegrating, with English nationalism increasing at the same time. None of this was inevitable of course, but it did suggest that the constitutional politics of the union would figure significantly in the post-Brexit world.

If Brexit provided the short answer to the question of Britain's recent political turbulence, there is also a longer answer. What had happened in Britain could not be disconnected from the rise of populist politics across Europe, with mainstream parties battered from both right and left in an insurgent attack on political elites. The issue of immigration in particular fuelled a populist nationalism. This in turn could not be disconnected from the fallout from the financial crash and the politics of austerity that followed. Britain's referendum on EU membership provided an opportunity for this populist surge to express itself. It had a distinctively British idiom of course, in terms of a view of its own history and attitude to the EU, but this should not obscure the connection to wider political trends. Indeed the reason why the EU was so anxious to contain the British exit was the fear of its contaminating effects in a volatile political environment.

If this provides the wider context, there is also a deeper context. Long before the EU referendum politics in Britain had been experiencing profound changes. The post-1945 generation had produced an account of British politics that held sway even as its foundations were being eroded. Its picture of a stable two-party system rooted in established political and class loyalties, producing uniform patterns of political behaviour across Britain, had ceased to be accurate. Where there was once stability, there was now fluidity. So too was the picture of a system of government that was uncomplicated and unrestrained. What had seemed to be the normal character of British politics turned out to be the exceptional product of a particular period. The story of this change can be told in many different ways, but its conclusion is clear. British politics had been on the move long before the 2016 referendum on EU membership.

In some ways it was even misleading still to refer to 'British politics' as a unitary phenomenon when it had come to take so many different forms. As John Curtice, the leading expert on electoral behaviour, has put it: 'In many respects now British general elections don't really happen and British politics doesn't really exist.' It was not just that Scotland had its own political system, as did Wales, different from the political system of England, but that everywhere political behaviour was less uniform and more variegated. The EU referendum had provided the most dramatic expression of this, as people and places divided on lines that confounded traditional loyalties. This presented a huge challenge for the old party system, and openings for new contenders (as the electoral impact of UKIP and the Brexit Party had shown for a time). British politics had experienced a seismic unsettlement; and it was impossible to know where it would eventually come to rest.

A new settlement of a kind had been achieved by Boris Johnson's emphatic victory in the election at the end of 2019. In settling the Brexit issue, with a departure date from the EU of 31 January

2020, it began the process of draining the poison out of British politics. There would still be plenty to argue about as a new trade relationship with the EU was negotiated, but the fact that Britain now had a stable majority government was crucial. After a decade in which governments had lacked secure majorities, the Conservative majority was unmatched since Mrs Thatcher's third victory in 1987. The electoral map had been redrawn. Labour had a leader who was widely seen as unelectable and it saw its heartland seats crumble in the face of Boris Johnson's pledge to 'get Brexit done' and break the parliamentary deadlock. The party suffered its worst defeat in terms of seats since 1935 and the worst in terms of vote share since its disastrous election of 1983.

The Conservative victory was the more remarkable since only a few months previously Brexit had threatened to inflict terminal damage on the party in a historic split. Its dramatic recovery was a reminder that the party believed above all else in power, and was quite prepared to remove one leader and install a more colourful one in order to achieve it. The fact that a government with a secure majority had been formed promised a return to some sort of political stability after a period of chaotic instability. Whether it represented a lasting realignment of British politics, along with the return of majority governments, or was merely the reflection of an exceptional set of circumstances, was a question for the future.

There were other questions too. Would the popular revolt that had produced Brexit continue to make its impact felt? Or would political argument return to the familiar distributional territory of taxing and spending between left and right? Had a politics of identity now replaced a politics of class? Would two-party political dominance continue to reassert itself or would fracturing and fragmentation continue? Would the major parties continue to hold their internal coalitions together? Would the habit of cross-party collaboration prompted by Brexit nourish a different kind of politics or would it be a return to business as usual? Would other parties, whether in the centre or on the extremes, gain ground? If governing without a majority had become the new normal, how would the conduct of politics change with the return of a government with a big majority? Might the case for electoral reform, and wider constitutional reform, grow stronger? Would the union survive? What would be the future impact of the generational divide? Would the causes of Brexit produce a sustained focus on the country's grievances and inequalities? Would the political engagement that Brexit had aroused continue or would distrust and disengagement intensify? Above all, what kind of country would Britain now become? Would it turn in on itself, its place in the world diminished, when it was no longer a member of a European bloc, or would it find a new role and confidence?

There were plenty of questions, but few clear answers. As ever, much turned on the balance between change and continuity. If the British political system had assumed its present form because of a continuous history without a decisive moment of rupture and reconstruction, then change might be the product of the decisive moment that Brexit represented. Yet the forces of continuity remained strong. For as long as the two major parties at Westminster believed they might form a majority government, they were unlikely to want to change the electoral system.

The prospect of getting agreement on the contents of a codified constitution seemed unlikely when agreement on anything had proved so difficult. Yet nothing was certain, and events might force the pace. The Johnson government arrived with its own ambitions to reorder the constitution, promising (vaguely, but in some eyes ominously) to review the relationship between government, parliament, and the courts. A political system that prided itself on its quality of adaptability had faced its sternest modern challenge. The fact that it had managed, against all the odds, to rescue itself from a period of acute instability might be seen as evidence of its ability to rise to this challenge. Yet, however much it might want to continue to muddle along, there might come a time when muddling along might no longer be enough.

This book began with an account of how political life in Britain had for a long time been seen as the exemplar of stable representative government. It ends with the political system beginning to recover from a period of crisis and disarray, as Brexit is finally digested. Strong government had become weak, but the decisive return of majority government in the 2019 election restored British politics to a traditional pattern that had seemed to have been lost. Whether this was to prove durable, or whether its eroded foundations would ensure future turbulence, only time would tell. If the traditional verdict on the British political system was that the executive was exceptionally powerful, the more recent verdict was that it had become exceptionally powerless. The old party system had seemed to be coming apart at the seams. Yet, suddenly and unexpectedly, strong government had reasserted itself and the familiar party system had remained intact.

There had been crisis before, from which new directions had emerged. The political cycle constantly turns; and endlessly surprises. In the 1970s there had been a crisis of governability, but this was a prelude to an enterprise of political reinvention. As Michael Moran has observed (in his *The End of British Politics?*), ever since the British state was created in 1707 'it has been reinvented by successive exercises in statecraft'. Brexit represents a pivotal turning point for the British polity, now joined in 2020 by the coronavirus crisis that is even more seismic in its impact and effect. It remains to be seen whether it finds its response in a new enterprise of creative statecraft.

Appendix

Table 2. General Election results (UK) since 1945: vote share and seats

Year	Con	Lab	LD	SNP/PC	Other
1945	39.7%/210	47.7%/393	9.0%/12	0.2%/0	3.4%/25
1950	43.3%/298	46.1%/315	9.1%/9	0.1%/0	1.4%/3
1951	48.0%/321	48.8%/295	2.6%/6	0.1%/0	0.6%/3
1955	49.6%/345	46.4%/277	2.7%/6	0.2%/0	1.1%/2
1959	49.4%/365	43.8%/258	5.9%/6	0.4%/0	0.6%/1
1964	43.3%/304	44.1%/317	11.2%/9	0.5%/0	0.9%/0
1966	41.9%/253	47.9%/364	8.5%/12	0.7%/0	1.0%/1
1970	46.4%/330	43.0%/288	7.5%/6	1.7%/1	1.5%/5
1974 (Feb.)	37.8%/297	37.2%/301	19.3%/14	2.6%/9	3.2%/14
1974 (Oct.)	35.7%/277	39.3%/319	18.3%/13	3.4%/14	3.3%/12
1979	43.9%/339	36.9%/269	13.8%/11	2.0%/4	3.4%/12

1983	42.4%/397	27.6%/209	25.4%/23	1.5%/4	3.1%/17
1987	42.2%/376	30.8%/229	22.6%/22	1.7%/6	2.7%/17
1992	41.9%/336	34.4%/271	17.8%/20	2.3%/7	3.5%/17
1997	30.7%/165	43.2%/418	16.8%/46	2.5%/10	6.8%/20
2001	31.6%/166	40.7%/412	18.3%/52	1.8%/9	7.7%/20
2005	32.4%198	35.2%/355	22.0%/62	2.2%/9	8.2%/22
2010	36.1%/306	29.0%/258	23.0%/57	2.2%/9	9.7%/20
2015	36.8%/330	30.4%/232	7.9%/8	5.3%/59	19.6%/21
2017	42.3%/317	40.0%/262	7.4%/12	3.6%/39	6.8%/20
2019	43.6%/365	32.2%/202	11.6%/11	4.4%/52	8.2%/20

Table 3. Governments formed after general elections (since 1945)

Year	Party	Prime minister	Majority
1945	Labour	Clement Attlee	147
1950	Labour	Clement Attlee	6
1951	Conservative	Winston Churchill	16
1955	Conservative	Anthony Eden (Harold Macmillan from 1957)	59
1959	Conservative	Harold Macmillan (Alec Douglas-Home from 1963)	99
1964	Labour	Harold Wilson	5
1966	Labour	Harold Wilson	97
1970	Conservative	Edward Heath	31
1974 (Feb.)	Labour	Harold Wilson	None
1974 (Oct.)	Labour	Harold Wilson (James Callaghan from 1976)	4
1979	Conservative	Margaret Thatcher	44
1983	Conservative	Margaret Thatcher	144
1987	Conservative	Margaret Thatcher (John Major from 1990)	101
1992	Conservative	John Major	21
1997	Labour	Tony Blair	178
2001	Labour	Tony Blair	166
2005	Labour	Tony Blair (Gordon Brown from 2007)	65

2010	Coalition (Con/LibDem)	David Cameron	77
2015	Conservative	David Cameron (Teresa May from 2016)	11
2017	Conservative	Teresa May (Boris Johnson from 2019)	None
2019	Conservative	Boris Johnson	80

Further reading

For those who want to explore British politics further, there is a huge volume of material available. All I can do here is to make some suggestions, with a bias towards readability (not an attribute of all political science literature) and an eye on the general reader.

A general overview is provided by the many excellent textbooks, aimed at different levels, although they can soon become out of date simply because of the pace of recent political developments. Useful textbooks include *Politics UK*, edited by Bill Jones, Philip Norton, and Oliver Daddow, 9th edn (Routledge, 2018); Simon Griffiths and Robert Leach, *British Politics*, 3rd edn (Macmillan, 2018); Michael Moran, *Politics and Governance in the UK*, 3rd edn (Macmillan, 2017); and Mark Garnett and Philip Lynch, *Exploring British Politics*, 4th edn (Routledge, 2017). These books are typically very chunky, with lots of student-friendly devices, and in some cases with companion websites. They also have extensive bibliographies, including the many journal articles which it is not possible to mention here. Apart from the specialist political science journals, two journals—*Political Quarterly* and *Parliamentary Affairs*—contain articles on British politics aimed at a more general readership.

There are two series of books which keep British politics under continuing review and are therefore particularly useful. *Developments in British Politics* (Palgrave Macmillan) tracks the changing political system. Its 10th edition was published in 2016 (ed. R. Heffernan et al.), so not able to cover recent developments, but previous editions are also worth consulting. The same applies to *The Changing*

Constitution series (OUP), the 9th edition of which (edited by Jowell and O'Cinneide) was published in 2019 and is invaluable for the analysis of constitutional developments.

A rich resource for students of British politics is the set of briefing papers produced by the House of Commons library. These are open access and so available to all (<http://www.parliament.uk>). The topic heading of 'parliament, government and politics' has authoritative briefings on many aspects of the political system, with reliable data, while other topic headings cover the range of policy areas. This material is highly recommended (and I have drawn on it for this book). There are a number of organizations, with websites and blogs, where British politics is analysed and discussed. These include the Hansard Society, the Constitution Unit at UCL, and the Institute for Government and Democratic Audit. The LSE British Politics and Policy blog is particularly useful in communicating in an accessible way.

I quote Walter Bagehot in this book, as writers on British politics often do. His *The English Constitution* (1867, several modern editions) is a classic of political writing and still deserves a place on any reading list. Anthony King's *The British Constitution* (OUP, 2007) is a Bagehot for our times. The same author's *Who Governs Britain?* (Pelican, 2015) is also recommended, not least for the clarity of its writing. Another minor classic is A. H. Birch, *Representative and Responsible Government* (Allen and Unwin, 1964), which provides a reminder of how British politics used to be understood. Anything by Peter Hennessy is worth reading, as an outstanding contemporary historian and explorer of the British state. His prolific output includes a book which influenced my own thinking, *The Hidden Wiring: Unearthing the British Constitution* (Gollancz, 1995), but there are many others. Also prolific is the constitutional historian Vernon Bogdanor (a long-time enthusiast for referendums), whose recent books include *The New British Constitution* (Hart, 2009) and *Beyond Brexit: Towards a British Constitution* (I.B. Tauris, 2019).

A vivid account of the 2016 referendum on EU membership that reshaped British politics is the journalist Tim Shipman's *All Out War* (Collins, 2017). Kevin O'Rourke's *A Short History of Brexit* (Pelican, 2019) provides useful background and context. There is a growing literature on the causes and consequences of Brexit in terms of changing political behaviour. Relevant books include Matthew

Goodwin and Robert Ford, *Revolt on the Right: Explaining Support for the Radical Right in Britain* (Routledge, 2014) and Harold Clarke, Matthew Goodwin, and Paul Whiteley, *Brexit: Why Britain Voted to Leave the European Union* (Cambridge, 2017). David Goodhart's *The Road to Somewhere: The Populist Revolt and the Future of Politics* (Hurst, 2017) tries to make sense of Britain's warring political tribes. Geoffrey Evans and Anand Menon, *Brexit and British Politics* (Polity, 2017) looks at what has been happening, and what might happen. The long-running British Election Study tracks changing electoral behaviour and forms the basis of Edward Fieldhouse, Jane Green, et al., *Electoral Shocks: The Volatile Voter in a Turbulent World* (OUP, 2019).

The members of Britain's political parties are analysed in Tim Bale, Paul Webb, and Monica Poletti, *Footsoldiers: Political Party Membership in the 21st Century* (Routledge, 2019). Reliable books on parliament are Philip Norton, *Parliament in British Politics* (2nd edn, Palgrave, 2013) and Nicolas Besly, Tom Goldsmith, Robert Rogers, and Rhodri Walters, *How Parliament Works* (8th edn, Routledge, 2018). The authority on the House of Lords (as well as parliament generally) is Meg Russell, most recently in *The Contemporary House of Lords: Westminster Bicameralism Revived* (OUP, 2013). Veteran Whitehall-watcher Peter Riddell's *15 Minutes of Power: The Uncertain Life of British Ministers* (Profile, 2019) takes the lid off the British way of governing, while Anthony King and Ivor Crewe, *The Blunders of our Governments* (updated edn, 2014, Oneworld) is a stylish and witty catalogue of policy failures (even before Brexit). It could be read alongside Margaret Hodge's *Called to Account* (Little Brown, 2017), based on her period chairing the Public Accounts Committee, which charts the difficulties of getting effective accountability for public money. For an insight into one of the spectacles of British politics, there is Ayesha Hazarika and Tom Hamilton, *Punch and Judy Politics: An Insiders' Guide to Prime Minister's Questions* (Biteback, 2018).

The increasing role of the judges in British politics, and the issues raised, will be informed by a reading of former top judge Tom Bingham's little masterpiece *The Rule of Law* (Penguin, 2013). Recent political history is vividly reviewed by Steve Richards, one of Britain's most acute political commentators, in his *The Prime Ministers: Reflections on Leadership from Wilson to May* (Atlantic, 2019). The 2018 Democratic Audit book *The UK's Changing*

Democracy (ed. Dunleavy, Park, and Taylor, LSE Press, 2018) evaluates political developments through a series of short chapters. Malcolm Dean, *Democracy under Attack: How the Media Distort Policy and Politics* (Policy Press, 2013) raises important issues. Michael Moran's essay *The End of British Politics?* (Palgrave, 2017) is outrageously priced but a stimulating read. The journalist Isabel Hardman's *Why We Get the Wrong Politicians* (Atlantic, 2018) is an interesting exploration of the political class. Also interesting is Philip Cowley and Robert Ford, *Sex, Lies and Politics* (Biteback, 2019), a witty collection of political nuggets. For those political anoraks who want more austere fare then *Butler's British Political Facts* (ed. Mortimore and Blick, Palgrave, 2018) provides it in abundance.

It is surprising (at least to me) that the academic literature on British politics frequently omits what politicians themselves have written about what they have been doing and observing. Of course this is often self-justifying, but it is also indispensable for giving a flavour of what political life in Britain is like. British politics has a rich reservoir of diarists and memoirists. Notable diarists of the post-war period include Richard Crossman, Barbara Castle, Alan Clark, and Tony Benn, while more recently there are the compulsively readable diaries of Chris Mullin and Alastair Campbell. Ruth Winstone's anthology of diarists, *Events, Dear Boy, Events: A Political Diary of Britain 1921 to 2010* (Profile, 2014) brings some of this material together. Recent prime ministerial memoirs are John Major, *The Autobiography* (Harper Collins, 2000), Tony Blair, *A Journey* (Hutchinson, 2010), and Gordon Brown, *My Life, Our Times* (Bodley Head, 2017). Among other recent political memoirs, Nick Clegg's *Between the Extremes* (Vintage, 2017) has interesting reflections on coalition government, while Ken Clarke's *Kind of Blue* (Pan, 2017) spans half a century of political life. Then, finally, there is David Cameron's *For the Record* (Collins, 2019) in which he has to explain why he was the architect of the 2016 referendum and all that has followed from it.

Index

For the benefit of digital users, indexed terms that span two pages (e.g., 52–53) may, on occasion, appear on only one of those pages.

AFRICAN HISTORY
A Very Short Introduction
John Parker & Richard Rathbone

Essential reading for anyone interested in the African continent and the diversity of human history, this *Very Short Introduction* looks at Africa's past and reflects on the changing ways it has been imagined and represented. Key themes in current thinking about Africa's history are illustrated with a range of fascinating historical examples, drawn from over 5 millennia across this vast continent.

'A very well informed and sharply stated historiography ... should be in every historiography student's kitbag. A tour de force ... it made me think a great deal.'

Terence Ranger,
The Bulletin of the School of Oriental and African Studies

www.oup.com/vsi

AMERICAN POLITICAL PARTIES AND ELECTIONS
A Very Short Introduction
Sandy L. Maisel

Few Americans and even fewer citizens of other nations understand the electoral process in the United States. Still fewer understand the role played by political parties in the electoral process or the ironies within the system. Participation in elections in the United States is much lower than in the vast majority of mature democracies. Perhaps this is because of the lack of competition in a country where only two parties have a true chance of winning, despite the fact that a large number of citizens claim allegiance to neither and think badly of both. Studying these factors, you begin to get a very clear picture indeed of the problems that underlay this much trumpeted electoral system.

www.oup.com/vsi

THE UNITED NATIONS
A Very Short Introduction
Jussi M. Hanhimäki

With this much-needed introduction to the UN, Jussi Hanhimäki
engages the current debate over the organization's effectiveness
as he provides a clear understanding of how it was originally
conceived, how it has come to its present form, and how it
must confront new challenges in a rapidly changing world. After
a brief history of the United Nations and its predecessor, the
League of Nations, the author examines the UN's successes
and failures as a guardian of international peace and security,
as a promoter of human rights, as a protector of international law,
and as an engineer of socio-economic development.

www.oup.com/vsi

THE EUROPEAN UNION
A Very Short Introduction
John Pinder & Simon Usherwood

This *Very Short Introduction* explains the European Union in plain English. Fully updated for 2007 to include controversial and current topics such as the Euro currency, the EU's enlargement, and its role in ongoing world affairs, this accessible guide shows how and why the EU has developed from 1950 to the present. Covering a range of topics from the Union's early history and the ongoing interplay between 'eurosceptics' and federalists, to the single market, agriculture, and the environment, the authors examine the successes and failures of the EU, and explain the choices that lie ahead in the 21st century.

www.oup.com/vsi

SOCIAL MEDIA
Very Short Introduction

Join our community
www.oup.com/vsi

- Join us online at the official Very Short Introductions **Facebook** page.
- Access the thoughts and musings of our authors with our online **blog**.
- Sign up for our monthly **e-newsletter** to receive information on all new titles publishing that month.
- Browse the full range of Very Short Introductions online.
- Read **extracts** from the Introductions for free.
- Visit our library of **Reading Guides**. These guides, written by our expert authors will help you to question again, why you think what you think.
- If you are a teacher or lecturer you can order inspection copies quickly and simply via our website.

ONLINE CATALOGUE
A Very Short Introduction

Our online catalogue is designed to make it easy to find your ideal Very Short Introduction. View the entire collection by subject area, watch author videos, read sample chapters, and download reading guides.

http://fds.oup.com/www.oup.co.uk/general/vsi/index.html